"*A Course in Desert Spirituality* offers keen insight into the wisdom of early Christian mystics like St. Gregory of Nyssa, John Cassian, and Evagrius Ponticus. It makes the D come alive. But it also reveals much at Thomas Merton himself."

— Carl McColman, author of *Th Mysticism* and *The Unteach.*

"As explored in this book, Christian tradition is embedded in desert spirituality. Merton's enduring voice takes us on a journey into the desert, allowing us to meet many Desert Mothers and Fathers, and grow in our own sense understanding about desert spirituality. In true Merton form, this book prompts insights and self-reflection. Another gift to the world in the Merton canon."

— Cassidy Hall, author of *Notes on Silence* and director of *Day of a Stranger*

"This fine book is filled with great insight and inspiration! Isn't it amazing that in this materialistic and superficial world, early desert spirituality would have so much to teach us today? And even more because it is filtered through the mind and heart of a true master teacher from our own time! This is very good food indeed."

— Fr. Richard Rohr, OFM, Center for Action and Contemplation, Albuquerque, New Mexico

A Course in Desert Spirituality

Fifteen Sessions
with the Famous Trappist Monk

Thomas Merton

Edited by
Jon M. Sweeney

Foreword by
Paul Quenon, OCSO

LITURGICAL PRESS
Collegeville, Minnesota

www.litpress.org

Cover design by Tara Wiese. Photo courtesy of Wikimedia Commons.

1	2	3	4	5	6	7	8	9

Library of Congress Cataloging-in-Publication Data

Names: Merton, Thomas, 1915–1968, author. | Sweeney, Jon M., 1967–
   editor.
Title: A course in desert spirituality : fifteen sessions with the famous
   Trappist monk / by Thomas Merton ; edited by Jon M. Sweeney.
Description: Collegeville, Minnesota : Liturgical Press, [2019] | Includes
   bibliographical references and index.
Identifiers: LCCN 2018048539| ISBN 9780814684733 (pbk.) | ISBN
   9780814684986 (eISBN)
Subjects: LCSH: Desert Fathers.
Classification: LCC BR67 .M467 2019 | DDC 271—dc23
LC record available at https://lccn.loc.gov/2018048539

"The world pursues us into the desert and seeks to win us back. If we have anything in us belonging to the world, the world has a claim on us." (Lecture 15)

Contents

Foreword

Paul Quenon, OCSO

The Desert Fathers were a special delight to Thomas Merton in his wide reading and research of the Church Fathers. One well-known photograph of him, by John Howard Griffin, shows him seated over a large tome, in a denim jacket, which was standard winter wear for all the monks; he is reading the volume and laughing at it. Upon closer inspection, you can discern the letters on the page were in a foreign language and one could easily conjecture it was the Migne Latin edition of the *Apothegmata*, the "Sayings" of the Desert Fathers.

Among the variety of conferences I attended by Fr. Louis in the Novitiate, the funniest were those about the Desert Fathers. The hermits' odd behaviors, their blunt, simple answers to spiritual seekers, were evocative of the short, salutary words of Jesus himself. Words practical, unexpected, maybe off-putting like: "Keep to your cell, and your cell will teach you all things." Or, "*Fuge, silere et tachere.*" "Flee, keep quiet and be silent." The exotic names of these peculiar men began to ring in our heads, as well: Paphnutius, Arsenius, Pachomius. We heard stories of their quasi-prophetic behavior, such as one hermit who walked into the gathering of monks as they deliberated on the eviction of one brother who had greatly sinned. Upon his shoulder this wise Father carried a bag of sand with a hole in the bottom, trailing sand across the floor. He declared: "I am another sinner and I leave a trail of sins behind me like this sand." After that, they decided to forgive and receive the wayward monk back into their midst. Unforgettable.

One of the chief concerns in this literature is "the discernment of spirits"; how do you know what inspirations come from God and what comes from the devil? John Cassian tells the sad story of Brother John who decided he would prove his faith by throwing himself down a well and show he suffered no harm. That he straightway did—and perished.

Merton, in *The Wisdom of the Desert*, his translation of the "Sayings," compared such tales to the Zen Buddhist masters, and one could as well include Shams Tabrizi, as recounted by Rumi. But one need look no further than the subsequent literature of the Greek and Cappadocian Fathers to see further flowering of that seminal inspiration of the desert monks: most remarkably Evagrius Ponticus, Basil, Gregory of Nazianzus, and extending westward, John Cassian and St. Benedict. While much of this later writing wafted on lengthy wings of rhetoric rather than on cryptic, monastic brevity, at its core it came from men envious of the simple, rustic lives of these solitaries. Most of the authors found in this current volume were wannabe monks, and probably at heart they really were, while being caught up in the complexities and conflicts of a church suffering growing pains in a Hellenic culture.

None of this history was unsuitable for us fledgling novices in a modern monastery, to sample and taste. St. Benedict, in his Rule for monks, recommends such readings in preference to his very own "little rule for beginners." In today's turbulent world many women and men in Europe, America, and Latin America are looking toward Benedictine and earlier traditions for a guide on how to live. They feel an urgent need for "discernment of spirits" on many fronts, personal, ecclesiastical, and political. How can we detect what is motivating people—myself, others, and those big faces on the TV screen? The path to "purity of heart," to unselfish, authentic, and guileless intentions of the mind and will, were understood by these wise and simple men and women of Egypt, Syria, and Palestine. Here they are carefully spelled out again for our guidance.

Editor's Prologue

As with this book's predecessor, *A Course in Christian Mysticism*, the volume you are holding originated in talks Thomas Merton gave to the novices at the Abbey of Gethsemani. And as with the earlier book, *A Course in Desert Spirituality* is redacted from previously published, scholarly editions.

Both *Courses* are attractive to those of us who live outside monasteries because of Merton's brilliant ability to survey the key figures and synthesize their writings, inspiring his listeners and readers with what it means for the spiritual life. But this *Course* is also attractive to non-monastics because of Merton's belief—which comes through clearly in the presentation—that monastic wisdom and spirituality are applicable for everyone. As Merton once said:

> [T]here is a monastic outlook which is common to all those who have elected to question the value of a life submitted entirely to arbitrary secular presuppositions, dictated by social convention, and dedicated to the pursuit of temporal satisfactions which are perhaps only a mirage. Whatever may be the value of "life in the world" there have been, in all cultures, men [and women] who have claimed to find something they vastly prefer in solitude.[1]

So if you are a person with the sort of "monastic outlook" that Merton describes so well, this book of fifteen lectures is for your

---

[1] Thomas Merton, *The Way of Chuang Tzu* (New York: New Directions, 1997), 10.

benefit—even though, perhaps especially because, it began as talks in a monastery.

In his first monastic decade, Merton began to struggle with life in community. This is one of the more intriguing narrative threads of every Merton biography. Books have been written specifically on this subject. We know how the dedicated Trappist sought greater solitude for himself, but also how he was one of the most loquacious spiritual writers of his generation. This irony and contradiction were not lost on anyone around Merton, not even on him.

Merton was frequently asking his abbot for more solitude, just as he was writing letters to hundreds of friends in the United States and abroad about every new book, every trending spiritual movement and idea. He was also actively talking to many of his desire for a more contemplative way of living. We even know of his yearning, at times, to transfer religious orders. If he were a Carthusian, could he better become the monk God wanted him to be? His later attraction to the religions and monastic traditions of the East are often seen in this light as well. There were even rumors after he died in Bangkok that he wasn't actually dead, but had faked his death in order to become a Buddhist monk and live in the East!

It was while studying John Cassian (the most important figure and teacher of these lectures) that Merton first gained permission for periods of greater solitude—and there are many moments in this book when we hear Merton arguing with the texts and the tradition (and himself? and his abbot?) on cenobitism vs. eremitism. The first is monastic life in community with other monks; the latter is the monastic life of hermits. Merton's abbot allowed him to make use of a wood shed on the monastery property for long afternoons and early evenings. Merton named the humble place "St. Anne's," and while maintaining his other commitments, he loved his time alone there. One early February in 1953, he wrote in his journal:

It is a tremendous thing no longer to have to debate in my mind about "being a hermit," even though I am not one. At least now solitude is something concrete—it is "St. Anne's"—the long view of hills, the empty cornfields in the bottoms, the crows in the trees, and the cedars bunched together on the hillside. And when I am here there is always lots of sky and lots of peace and I don't have distractions and everything is serene. . . .

Here there seems to be less and less need even of books.

Cassian has become tremendous, in a site which makes him irritable.[2]

That last line in the entry is a bit confusing, since Cassian drew his spiritual guidelines for monks—captured in his book of *Conferences*, the focus of Lectures 13 and 14 here—from encounters with, and admiration for, the lives and sayings of the Desert Fathers and Mothers, who were hermits. It was St. Benedict and his famous *Rule*, soon thereafter, that normalized cenobitism throughout Western monasticism. What do we make of that last line in the journal entry? I'm not sure. Perhaps it reveals some of Merton's own ambivalence or unease with his desire for solitude, which were sometimes very strong in him.

In these pages, you will discover much that is attractive, and some that's occasionally odd and unfortunate, in the lives and teachings and characters of those who left cities such as Alexandria, Damascus, and Jerusalem to seek greater faithfulness and commitment in the way of Christ. Merton demonstrates over and over movement in these two directions (attractive and unfortunate), and each was interesting to him. Particularly in

[2] Thomas Merton, *A Search for Solitude: Pursuing the Monk's True Life (The Journals of Thomas Merton, Vol. 3: 1952–1960)*, ed. Lawrence S. Cunningham (New York: HarperCollins, 1997), 29.

Lecture 2, on "Aberrations," he shows how we have seen developments in our spiritual understandings since the days of the early church. Montanism, for instance, with its combined "false asceticism and false mysticism," claimed an important Church Father (Tertullian) and is now understood as tragic. And the "hatred of the flesh" of Encratism, exhibited in heretical moments and occasionally in the genuine lives of Desert Fathers, isn't something to be emulated. Merton points both to ways in which we need to recapture and rediscover what was practiced long ago, and to what we've thankfully left behind.

I vividly remember encountering the treasure trove of lectures that Merton gave to the young men studying to become Trappist monks at The Abbey of Gethsemani in Kentucky. I'm old enough that I recall this first encounter via cassette tapes in the college library. The recording wasn't always clear, and I remember hitting stop, rewind, and play over and over to "catch" the wisdom in these nuggets. More than thirty years later, working with this material in written form has been a way of returning both to Merton and his sources, and to my own discovery of Merton—and that's been a joy.

For those who are interested in exploring Merton's teaching on desert spirituality in more detail, the unabridged, fully annotated versions of Merton's original novitiate conferences on this topic, accompanied by extensive introductions, are available in *Cassian and the Fathers: Initiation into the Monastic Tradition*, ed. Patrick F. O'Connell (Kalamazoo, MI: Cistercian Publications, 2005) and *Pre-Benedictine Monasticism: Initiation into the Monastic Tradition 2*, ed. Patrick F. O'Connell (Kalamazoo, MI: Cistercian Publications, 2006).

As O'Connell wrote in the introduction to that first volume: "While packed with factual and interpretive material, the conferences' focus was on formation rather than information. Their purpose was not to have the novices master a body of knowledge but to immerse them in a tradition, to allow them to become acclimated to a way of life that reached back in a continuous line to the early centuries of the Church." This is another way of explaining how and why these lectures are now relevant more than a half century after Thomas Merton's death.

There is the hope and possibility that the spirituality of the desert might form us—even those who have not taken monastic or religious vows—into better followers of Christ.

As such, this is not a book to be read casually. What the Desert Fathers and Mothers did with their lives, and how they interpreted the meaning of the Gospel, was never trivial and was not simple. To pick up this book is to study—but more than to study, it is to listen, and carefully. That should be the intention of all who read beyond this point.

As with *A Course in Christian Mysticism*, these are mysteries that you shouldn't attempt to encounter until you are prepared to meet them with your life. These lectures are not meant to be merely interesting; they are meant to transform. That's what Thomas Merton meant for them when they were first delivered, and his passion for that life and its relevance for life today comes through clearly.

From this point on, other than footnotes and backmatter, everything you will read is by Thomas Merton.

Jon M. Sweeney
The Feast of St. Francis of Assisi

Preface

If for some reason it were necessary for you to drink a pint of water taken out of the Mississippi River and you could choose where it was to be drawn out of the river—would you take a pint from the source of the river in Minnesota or from the estuary at New Orleans? This example is perhaps not perfect. Christian tradition and spirituality certainly do not become polluted with development. That is not the idea at all. Nevertheless, tradition and spirituality are all the more pure and genuine in proportion as they are in contact with the original sources and retain the same content.

Pius XII insisted that religious strive for renewal of their own authentic tradition, by a return to sources. Monastic spirituality is especially traditional and depends much on return to sources—to Scripture, Liturgy, Fathers of the Church.

Monastic life is the earliest form of religious life. The monk by his vocation belongs to the earliest kind of Christian spirituality. The original monastic sources have contributed to the stream of spirituality that has branched out in all the other orders; but the monk should get the life-giving waters from his proper source and not channeled through other spiritualities of later date, which have in them elements that are alien to the monastic life.

Besides renewal of our own tradition we must of course adapt ourselves to the needs of our time, and a return to tradition does not mean trying to revive, in all its details, the life lived by the early monks, or trying to do all the things that they did. It means living in our time and solving the problems of our time in the way and with the spirit in which they lived in a different time and solved different problems.

The primary concern of the desert life is to seek God, to seek salvation. The salutation common among Desert Fathers was "*sotheis*"—mayest thou be saved. Many of the sentences [we have come to know as their Sayings] are simply answers to the question, "What ought I to do?"

The Desert Fathers [and Mothers] were not necessarily magic directors, wizard gurus, who had a series of infallible answers on all points. They were humble and sagacious men [and women], of few words, whom the Holy Ghost used for His purposes.[1]

(1956)

---

[1] Merton doesn't use the phrase "Desert Mothers" in these lectures, for whatever reason. He uses the more common "Desert Fathers." Only in this first instance, for purposes of adding this editor's note, has the editor added "and Mothers" in editor's brackets. You will see, however, that Merton does discuss women, in addition to men—most of all in Lecture 9.

Early Christian Spirituality (First and Second Centuries)

These were the days of the great persecutions. The Christian was above all confronted at any moment with martyrdom. This is the keynote to the spirituality of the first centuries. Together with martyrdom as an ever-present possibility and conceived as the summit of the spiritual life, was also the ideal of virginity.

Martyrdom and virginity were considered as supreme forms of union with Christ by the sacrifice of all that the world holds dear. Asceticism went with this, hand in hand. The idea was, in all literal fact, to take up one's cross and follow Christ into the Kingdom where He reigns in glory. The Christian had no perspectives in this present life.

The life of the Christian was centered in the unity of the Church—a unity of perfect love, in which everything was still very much in common, and in which the Sacred Liturgy, the reenactment of the Redemptive Sacrifice of Christ, was the great communal act, the source of all strength, life, courage to face martyrdom, etc. The life of the Christian was an intense life of love and self-forgetfulness in the community of the faithful, closely united together in Christ by the Liturgy, and daily expecting to bear witness to their faith in Christ by death.

In this situation there was not much literature, not much "pious reading." What was written was written to be read to the community, or for the formation of catechumens. Examples include St. Ignatius and his epistles, *The Didache* or "Teaching" (of the Twelve Apostles), [and] the *Shepherd of Hermas* (allegorical and apocalyptic visions). Note that the spirituality of the early church was strongly eschatological. [For example], in *The Didache*: "There are two ways, one of life and one of death; and great is the difference between the two ways" (opening words). The way of life is simply the way of the Gospel and in summarizing it the author repeats and summarizes the main moral teachings of Jesus, quoted from the Gospel. For instance:

> This is the way of life: "First you shall love God who made you, secondly, your neighbor as yourself; and whatever you would not like done to you, do not do to another." The teaching of these words is as follows: "Bless those who curse you, and pray for your enemies, and fast for those who persecute you. For what is the merit of loving those who love you? Do not even the pagans do this? But, love those who hate you, and you will not have an enemy."

Read especially chapters 9 and 10 on the Eucharist—beautiful, simple, deep—[these are] the first beginnings of the liturgy in spontaneous prayer. We should keep this spirit and spontaneity in our own worship. Chapter 10 is a model for the Mass, and can also be [a] model for our own prayer after communion.

[Then there was] St. Ignatius of Antioch, the second successor to St. Peter as Bishop of Antioch, an important city. His writings are marked by ardent love for Christ, love for unity of the Church, thirst for martyrdom. Study his conception of the Church and of the Christian life. Read his desire for martyrdom. Hence the spirituality of the age of the martyrs can be summed up as follows.

Spirituality in the Age of the Martyrs

1) Everything is centered in the unity of the Mystical Christ: humility and meekness and the virtues that promote unity

are paramount, and above all *charity*. From the *Epistle of Clement*:

> Make us submissive to Thy most mighty and excellent name, to our princes and governors in this world. For Thou, O Master, hast given them the power of reigning by Thy glorious and unspeakable might, in order that, knowing the glory and honour Thou hast assigned to them, we should obey them and not contradict Thy will. O Lord, grant unto them health, peace, concord, and stability, that they may wield without hindrance the sovereignty which Thou hast given them. For Thou, Master, and heavenly King of all the ages, givest unto the sons of men glory, honour and power over the things of the earth. Guide Thou, O Lord, their counsels according to that which is good, according to that which is pleasing in Thy sight, so that they may use with reverence in peace and mildness the power which Thou hast given them, and enjoy Thy favor (Prayer for the Roman emperors by Clement and the Roman Christians in their liturgical gatherings).

2) Special emphasis is put on the mystique of martyrdom—the consummation of the Christian's consecration of himself to Christ in baptism. Tertullian writes: "A prison provides a Christian with the same advantages that a desert gives to a prophet." This is interesting. Not only are the Desert Fathers heirs to the vocation of the martyrs, but the martyrs are the heirs of those pre-desert fathers, the prophets. In either case, there is the idea of the *prophetic* vocation of the Christian saint as witness to the presence of Christ in the world (classic example—St. John the Baptist, model of martyrs, of monks, and of prophets). Tertullian encourages martyrs in strength and love of suffering for Christ:

> Blessed martyrs, look upon every hardship you have to endure as fitted to develop in you virtues of soul and body. You are about to take up the good fight in which the living God will award the prize. . . . Christ Jesus, who has anointed

you with the Holy Spirit, has willed before the day of battle to take away your freedom and to deal with you stoutly to toughen your strength. Athletes, as we know, in order to harden themselves, withdraw from their fellows to undergo a regime of greater severity. They abstain from all indulgence, all dainty fare, and all too pleasant drink. They do themselves violence, undergo pain, tire themselves out, being surer of winning the more thoroughly they are trained. And yet all this is, as the Apostle says [1 Cor. 9:25] "that they may receive a corruptible crown: but we an incorruptible one." Let us then regard the prison as the place where we are trained to suffer, that we may be broken in to it when we are led forth to the tribunal. For a hard life increases virtue, softness on the contrary destroys it.

St. Cyprian writes in his *Exhortation to Martyrs*: "The world becomes a prison, in time of persecution: but the heavens are opened. Antichrist threatens but Christ comes to the rescue; death is inflicted, but immortality follows; the martyr who is put to death loses the world, but restored to life he gains paradise. Temporal life is snuffed out but eternal life is given in exchange."

Typical of the spirit of the martyrs, this strength and love of sacrifice is passed on and handed down by the martyr to the monk his successor. How necessary to have some of this spirit in our monastic life. Otherwise how feeble and inert we will be, how lacking in generosity, how tepid in fulfilling our sacred obligations.

The age of the martyrs looked at union with Christ Crucified, by martyrdom, as the ideal way of fulfilling one's vocation to union with Christ and swallowing up all sin and burying sin and punishment alike in the Blood of Christ. But not all were martyrs—nor was it sufficient to hope for martyrdom as the exclusive and unique way of being a perfect Christian. What if one did not die a martyr? How should one live? One should live as if preparing for martyrdom. But the Christian virtues should be practiced in a very special way by certain groups within the Church.

The Ideal of Virgins and Ascetes

The life of virginity is also a life of union with Christ. The virgin is the Bride of Christ. Those who embrace the life of virginity do not merely renounce marriage and legitimate pleasures of the flesh, but in general they embrace lives of greater mortification. While all the faithful fast on Wednesday and Friday, these have an even stricter rule of life. "We often meet with Christians who might marry and thus spare themselves the aggravation of the struggle between the flesh and the spirit. They prefer to refrain from exercising their right, but to lay upon themselves hard penances, to keep under their bodies by fasting, to bring them under obedience by abstinence from certain foods, and thus in every way to mortify by the spirit the works of the flesh," wrote Origen.

Since perfect chastity is a special gift of God, then it must be asked for and preserved by a life of constant prayer. But prayer is not only associated with the virginal life because of its difficulties. Also, the life of virginity fits one to offer special praise to God. It becomes a life of praise, a life devoted (later on) to the *opus Dei.* The virgins follow the Lamb singing hymns wherever He goes. Apocalypse 14:1-6:

> And I saw, and behold, the Lamb was standing upon Mount Sion, and with him a hundred and forty-four thousand having his name and the name of his Father written on their foreheads. And I heard a voice from heaven like a voice of many waters, and like a voice of loud thunder; and the voice that I heard was as of harpers playing on their harps. And they were singing as it were a new song before the throne, and before the four living creatures and the elders; and no one could learn the song except those hundred and forty-four thousand, who have been purchased from the earth. These are they who were not defiled with women; for they are virgins. These follow the Lamb wherever he goes. These were purchased from among men, first-fruits unto God and unto the Lamb, and in their mouth there was found no lie; they are without blemish.

It is especially fitting that pure souls should devote themselves to the praise of God—they are able to love and understand
Him better; they are on more intimate terms with Him; praise
in the mouth of a pure person is more pleasing to God, etc. This
life of prayer early took the form of an embryonic divine office:
all Christians assisted at vigils of reading and psalmody in church
from Saturday to Sunday (from this arose the office of matins).
Virgins and ascetes habitually prayed at set times of the day,
especially morning, noon and evening. The prayer life of all was
centered, of course, in the Holy Eucharistic sacrifice.

The life of prayer and penance was also accompanied by good
works. Virgins and ascetes were assigned officially to certain
works of mercy in the Church, as part of their vocation. Hence
the virginal life is the angelic life, a special spiritual gift coming
down from heaven. But it must be accompanied with humility
and works of charity. (St. John Chrysostom will later point out
that the foolish virgins with no oil in their lamps lacked works
of mercy and were attached to their possessions.) The pure love
of the virgins, far from being sterile, is spiritually fecund (*gloriosa
fecunditas*) in the Church, not only spiritually but even tempo-
rally. St. Ambrose was to say later: "Where virgins are few in
number there the population diminishes, but where virginity is
held in honor there too the number of inhabitants increases,"
and he refers to Alexandria as an example.

Aberrations in the Early Centuries

𝕴n order to understand the Christian tradition of the early centuries we must also know about the aberrations from the true tradition, which had a significant effect. We have to be careful in studying such things: not because we are likely to be led astray by the errors themselves, but because we are apt to make judgements that are too crude both of the nature of error and of the nature of true Christian spirituality. There is a danger of drawing very clear lines of demarcation, with all black on one side and all white on the other, and so a need for greater discernment. For instance, much that was good in Neoplatonism has in fact passed over to the Fathers, for example St. Augustine.

Hatred of the Flesh

Encratism (from *egkrateia*—abstaining), exaggerated asceticism—hatred of the flesh—is not Christian. This error condemned all marriage and all use of meat and wine as evil. On the contrary, St. Methodius gives the true doctrine: "In marriage God associates man with His own creative work."

True asceticism supposes a balance: perfection consists not in denying oneself but in charity. Asceticism is a means to an end and not an end in itself. Eusebius gives an example of true Christian spirit in the martyr Alcibiades of Lyons. In prison, he was severely abstaining from certain foods. But when it was pointed out that this was troubling others who thought they might be obliged to do the same, he "made use of everything indifferently, thanking God, for the martyrs were not bereft of the grace of God, but the Holy Spirit was their counsellor."

Tatian and Encratism

Tatian was an Assyrian convert in Rome. At first interested in Greek philosophy, he turned against it and remained aggressively opposed to Greek influence in Christianity. In a rigorous opposition against Western Christianity, he emphasized extreme asceticism for all and even opposed marriage and procreation. He was condemned as a heretic in the West. He had a decisive influence in Syrian Christianity. Note his *Gospel Harmony* [which shows] examples of the way Tatian changed Gospel texts to suit his own rigorous views. He excluded wine from the Kingdom, omitted references to Joseph as Mary's "husband," etc. Note: Jerome, commenting on Galatians 6:8 ("He who sows in the flesh . . .") attributes to a most zealous heresiarch of the Encratists, Cassianus, the view that this is a text against marriage. This Cassianus may be "Tatianus" (an error of the scribe) or else Julian Cassianus, a Valentinian gnostic. Defending fasting against Jovinian, Jerome mentions Tatian and Marcion as heretics who forbade certain foods out of "hatred for the works of the creator." The true Christian view: "We give praise for every creature of God"—but Christians fast nevertheless. Fasting is commanded by Christ, but not because any creature is evil. Tatian places great emphasis on suffering in the spiritual life.

Marcionites

As a result of dualism, Marcion separated the "good God" of the New Testament and the evil principle of the Old Testament. Creation comes from the evil one. Hence to despise creation is to insult and contemn the evil principle. Marriage was treated with nausea. Only celibates could be full members of the

Church (cf. Albigenses). Marcion taught a hatred of the body, a Docetist view of the Incarnation and made the claim that Christ hated the flesh. He taught hatred of food: eating is regarded as a bestial and evil action. Marcionites showed aggressive opposition to the world, courting persecution.

The Acts of Thomas (Apocryphal)

This work shows a modified encratism, with an emphasis on virginity. Only the virgins are espoused to Christ, and they alone can enter with Him into the Kingdom. It is also necessary to leave all possessions, for Christ comes only to those who are stripped of all things. Vagrancy is praised. In these sources and others (cf. the Apocryphal *Odes of Solomon*) we see ascesis regarded as an essential part of the Christian message. The Gospel is only for those who practice extreme asceticism.

The idea was eschatological: the refusal of procreation had a cosmic significance. It was supposed to hasten the day of the end. The celibate took a real and concrete part in the "reduction of the dominion and duration of the present world." "Only a church with such qualities could be an instrument working towards the consummation of the cosmic upheaval and the expansion of God's dominion in the world." Hence the sacraments were rewards for the continent (for example, Baptism as a crown for the perfect, not an initiation).

Encratism:

1) It is dualistic, rejects the Old Testament and ascribes the division of the sexes to the demon.

2) Therefore it prescribed total abstention from marriage and meat.

3) A "metaphysical hatred of wine" was carried to the point that water only was used at Mass.

Tatian [also] taught that Adam was not saved because he married.

St. Basil's Master, Eustathius

Eustathius was St. Basil's friend and guide, who introduced him to the full ascetic ideal, and urged him to go to Egypt. Basil long remained under the influence of Eustathius but gradually came to differ with him.

Eustathius [was] Bishop of Sebaste (Armenia), who had travelled in Egypt, admired the monks, propagated asceticism in Asia Minor, [and] had many followers and many opponents. The left wing of Eustathius' following tended toward heresy and exaggerated asceticism, preparing the way for Messalianism. The influence of Eustathius precipitated a crisis reflected in the Council (Synod) of Gangres in 341, more than ten years before Basil came under his direct influence, though Basil's family embraced ascetic life under the influence of Eustathius about ten years after the council. At the Council of Gangres, opposition to Eustathius by conservative elements in the Church crystallized in a "condemnation" of Eustathius or rather of the extreme tendencies which some of his followers promoted. From this council it is clear that the left-wing Eustathians tended toward schism, asserting that only the perfect ascetics were worthy [of] the name of true Christians. Married clergy were despised. The hierarchy was condemned for compromising with the world of imperial power. Ascetes were accused of disrupting the social order, breaking up marriages, urging slaves to flee masters and officials to leave jobs to become monks. Monks refused to pay taxes, etc. Ascetes were accused of contempt for the ordinary liturgical life of the Church, feasts of martyrs (which tended to be social festivities), contempt for created things, etc. Extremists on the other hand found that Eustathius himself was not strict enough. Some of the ascetes protested against his foundation of a hospital at Sebaste as a source of distractions and worldliness. They departed into the mountains with a group of men and women bound to celibate and ascetic life. These extremists, as later the Messalians, exalted the life of prayer beyond all else; prayer supplied for everything, better than work. They also practiced sacred dances and preached "liberation of women."

Rather than saying that St. Basil reacted against Eustathian ascesis, it would be better to say that St. Basil took what he considered best and most evangelical in the doctrine and practice of his master, and affirmed it, as against the extremism of the left wing, which involved total separation from the ordinary faithful, condemning them as un-Christian. After the Council of Gangres, St. Basil emphasized what was genuine and truly traditional in the doctrine and practice of Eustathius, and worked out a way of life for all Christians to be perfect, according to the teaching of the Gospel. This way of life was not strictly speaking monastic life—though tradition regarded it as such. If by monastic life is meant withdrawal from the ordinary Christian community as well as from the world, then Basil was not "legislating for the monastic life." If by monastic life is meant ascetic communities within and in contact with the Christian community as a whole, then this is what Basil envisaged! He is talking of what we mean today by the religious life—especially that of active congregations, rather than of "contemplative monks." The love of money and rank were to be renounced, along with the love of pleasure, comfort, etc. Emphasis was placed on a life of prayer and work, as opposed to the one-sided emphasis on prayer preached by the extremists.

Montanism

Montanism was the great heresy of the second century. It claimed Tertullian as one of its adherents. In it false asceticism and false mysticism were combined. It contains elements common in movements of similar type down the ages:

1) Crude idea of eschatology: the end of the world is about to happen any day now.

2) The reign of the Holy Spirit had begun. Hence there is an obligation for all to practice extreme asceticism.

3) Perfection consists in extraordinary mystical gifts and experience. Montanus was a priest with his two prophetesses,

Priscilla and Maximilla. Frequency of visions and ecstatic madness, spectacular manifestations of "possession by the Holy Spirit," convulsions, etc. marked the movement, which was condemned by the Church.

Neoplatonism

The above were heretical movements. Neoplatonism is not a Christian deviation; it is a Hellenistic philosophical and mystical school of thought. It falls short of Christianity and was opposed to it, but it cannot be dismissed lightly. It flourished at Alexandria; Plotinus, Proclus, etc. were its main lights. It represented a development of Plato's philosophy with religious elements from the Near East included; thus it was syncretistic. Much of the Christian tradition on "contemplation" is in fact full of the influence of Neoplatonism.

The word "contemplation" does not occur in the Gospel. The idea of abstracting oneself from all things, purifying one's mind of all images, and ascending by self-denial to an ecstatic intellectual contact with God the Supreme Truth—ending up by being "alone with the alone"—all this is characteristic of the Neoplatonic approach. It has been taken over by a whole tradition of Christian writers and has become Christianized. But still we must remember in dealing with such writers that we are handling a characteristically Greek type of thought and must take care not to lose sight of Christ Himself and His teachings in order to follow a more or less pagan line of thought from which Christ is all but excluded.

One specifically Neoplatonic element is the idea that contemplation (*gnosis*) is for a select elite and others cannot attain it. It is true St. Paul speaks of perfect Christians and carnal-minded Christians—but that is not quite the same thing.[1]

---

[1] See, for instance, 1 Cor. 2:6, 3:1, 14:20; Eph. 4:13; Col. 1:28, 4:12.

Another element is dualism, in which body and soul are considered as separated: soul belongs to the realm of spirit, body to the realm of matter, and the material is inferior if not even evil. Origen was led astray by this idea. Hence arises the conclusion that to live a "purely spiritual" life is better; hence also the emphasis on *apatheia* (complete freedom from passion) as the climax of ascetic life. Nowhere in the New Testament do we find such an ideal of complete deliverance of the soul from the body. On the contrary, the New Testament envisages the spiritualization of the whole man, body and soul together, pointing to the Resurrection of the Flesh. But ideas like *apatheia* became part and parcel of Christian ascetic theory and practice, especially in the Orient. They must always be qualified with Christian correctives.

Gnosticism

Gnosticism [is] a deviation from Christianity (an attempt to "improve" on it), cruder, more oriental, more elaborate than Neoplatonism. It was also more esoteric (that is, salvation and sanctification are more exclusively for an elite of initiates). There is a very curious mythological and magical content in Gnosticism, which posited a "Pleroma" of mythical personages, some friendly to God and some inimical to him. Note the creation of personages like "Sabaoth" due to misunderstanding of the Septuagint. (They thought the Lord Sabaoth [Lord of Armies] was a special personage called "Sabaoth"—a kind of demiurge.) However Gnosticism is centered on Jesus. A fantastic ascent through the thirteen aeons brings the perfect soul at last to Jesus himself, the supreme Mystery of Light, above all the celestial archons.

Gnosticism was an attempt to unite Christianity with astrology and magic, rejecting the Old Testament and substituting for it the pseudo-sciences of the day. Dualism was present even in divine things: God of the Old Testament was evil (enemy of Jesus), God of the New Testament good; body was evil, "tomb" of the soul, etc. The universe came from an evil principle called Ialdaboth. These ideas were taken up by Manichaeans later.

We can recognize similar trends all down through the history of the Church. Such trends arise when there are times of unrest, when the masses are spiritually hungry and going through a period of transition. Such trends are associated with ignorance (excluding Neoplatonism of course) and misinterpretation of Christian revelation—and with relatively crude natural appetites for spiritual experience. They flare up and lead to many excesses, but when they die down the spirit of whole classes or groups is left "burnt out" and helpless.

The Christian Teachers of Alexandria

I t is very important to know something of this great school. The work of this school was the establishment of Christianity as a spiritual and intellectual movement acceptable to the upper classes and to the intellectuals.

Clement of Alexandria

Clement and Origen adopted as much of Greek thought as could be harmonized with Christianity. Note—the large and influential Jewish colony at Alexandria included many intellectuals who for generations had been working to reconcile Platonism and Jewish thought. Clement interpreted Exodus 11:1-3, about borrowing precious vessels from the Egyptians, in the sense that the Church should appropriate all that was good in pagan philosophy. In this he followed an interpretation already favored by the Alexandrian Jews. At the same time Clement believed that Plato, Socrates, etc. had been saved by their knowledge of God arrived at through philosophy. Knowledge was their "covenant" as the Law was the covenant of the Jews. Tertullian on the contrary thought Greek philosophy came from the devil.

Clement considers the Christian life as a progress from faith to gnosis. In this he is perhaps too intellectual and remains too close to pagan philosophical terms. He wrote three books, guides to the Christian life, presenting Christ in three aspects:

1) The *Protreptikos* (Converter)—How the Lord converts souls and awakens them to the new life of faith: an apologia of Christianity for the Greeks.

2) The *Paidagogos* (Teacher of Small Children)—Christ teaches and guides us in the beginnings and ordinary paths of Christianity. Written for "Christians in the world," it throws many lights on the social life of Alexandria in the second century. See quotes from the *Paidagogos* about food, for example: [When invited to dinner, the Christian should eat what is set before him, as Paul recommends] "We are not, then, to abstain wholly from various kinds of food, but only are not to be taken up about them. We are to partake of what is set before us, as becomes a Christian, out of respect to him who has invited us, by a harmless and moderate participation in the social meeting." [And], "it is the mark of a silly mind to be amazed and stupefied at what is presented at vulgar banquets, after the rich fare which is in the Word."[1]

3) The *Stromata*—Clement's greatest work. *Stromata* means "Carpets" [and] consists in various unsystematic thoughts— especially on the relation of Christian wisdom to pagan learning. Pagan philosophy paves the way for Christ. In it Clement also argues against gnostics and opposes to them the true Christian gnosis. In his ascetic teaching Clement insisted too much on the division between the ordinary Christian and the "gnostic" (contemplative), and also demanded that the perfect Christian be completely above all passion (*apatheia*).

---

[1] Merton found these quotes from Clement in Anne Fremantle, ed., *A Treasury of Early Christianity* (New York: Viking Press, 1953), 49, 50.

Origen

There is a kind of fashion among superficial minds to dismiss Origen as a heretic and have nothing to do with him. This is very unfortunate because Origen is certainly one of the greatest and even holiest of the Church Fathers and was certainly the most influential of the early Fathers. His contribution to Catholic theology and spirituality was inestimable, and if he unfortunately did fall into theological errors (which was not to be wondered at in these early times when theological teaching had not been at all systematized), it is not difficult to separate his errors from the great mass of his orthodox teaching.

Of all the Eastern Fathers Origen is perhaps the one who remained the most influential in Western monasticism, not excluding St. Basil. St. Bernard's commentary on the Canticle of Canticles, which is typical of the whole theology and spirituality of the Cistercians and of medieval monasticism as a whole, goes back directly to Origen, and is often merely an elaboration of the basic ideas found in Origen (many of which in turn go back to Philo Judaeus).

Origen was born in 185 of Christian parents; his father Leonidas died as a martyr under Severus (202). Origen was prevented by a trick from offering himself up to the persecutors; his mother hid all his clothes. He lost all his patrimony in the persecution, and at eighteen he began teaching in the school of Alexandria, abandoned by Clement.

The Catechetical School of Alexandria grew up on the confines of the great pagan university—it had been started by a converted Stoic, Pantaenus (a kind of Newman Club)—converts were instructed, curious pagans came for lectures, Christians were prepared for Orders. The master received pupils in his own house. For some, simple study of the Creed was enough. Others received a full intellectual training in science, philosophy, letters—with an apologetic slant. The course culminated in ethics, where dialectical training began—questions, for example good and evil, leading up to theology. According to Eusebius he lived a life of strict asceticism and evangelical poverty, fasted, slept on the floor. However, in misguided ascetic zeal he castrated himself: a grave error.

At first he taught secular subjects—dialectics, physics, mathematics, astronomy, Greek philosophy—and attracted pagans by these courses. Later he devoted himself entirely to Christian theology.

In 216, he moved to Palestine. Not yet ordained, he was invited to preach (as distinguished from teach). This created a scandal in Alexandria: his bishop opposed it. The bishops in Palestine ordained Origen. Demetrius of Alexandria protested that the ordination was illicit since Origen had castrated himself, and excommunicated Origen. The bishop of Caesarea adopted him and ignored the excommunication; Origen continued to teach at Caesarea. Origen was imprisoned and tortured under Decius, and died at Tyre in 253 as a result of his sufferings. In effect, he gave his life for the faith. But he had many enemies during life and many after death.

There was a storm about Origenism about 400 and finally the Council of Constantinople in 543 anathematized certain propositions of Origen. His errors are due to his excessive Platonism. His main errors condemned by the Church concern:

1) The pre-existence of the human soul

2) The Resurrection—the manner of the resurrection of the body

3) The *apocatastasis*—that Christ will somehow renew His Passion for the demons and the damned and that the punishments of hell will be brought to an end

As a result of the controversies, much of his original writing disappeared, and what remains was largely preserved in Latin. There were supposed to have been between two and six thousand treatises by him in existence.

Origen's Writings

His works on Scripture include *The Hexapla*: [a] six-column translation (original Hebrew, Hebrew in Greek characters, and four Greek translations annotated by Origen). And, *Commentaries*—Origen, the first great Christian exegete, commented on practically every book of the Old and New Testaments. The commentaries are often in the form of homilies addressed to the people, but are generally deep and mystical. Origen is a master of the spiritual, mystical or typological sense of Scripture, and also is rich in tropological (moral) interpretations of the sacred books. His writings on Scripture are, with his treatise *On Prayer*, the most important for monks. His scriptural commentaries are rich and full of inexhaustible ideas, as long as we do not expect from him *scientific* interpretations. But his mystical interpretations are not mere fancy and subjectivism. He treats the Scriptures as a whole new world of types and symbols, and the end result is a contemplative wisdom, a broad, rich, penetrating view of the universe as "sacrament" and "mystery" in Christ, for which there is plenty of warrant in the New Testament.

Other important works are:

1) *De Principiis*—the fundamentals of knowledge, especially as a basis for theology.

2) *On Prayer*—the oldest Christian treatise on prayer, in two parts. It deals with prayer in general, the validity of petition; and the Our Father (a commentary). Conditions for true prayer [include that] one must be earnestly striving to detach himself from sin; one must be struggling to become free from domination by the passions, especially those which cause conflict with our neighbor; [and] one must strive to avoid distractions. But after all one must remember that *prayer is a gift of the Holy Ghost*. Origen recommended that we pray standing, facing east: (Christ = rising sun).

3) *Contra Celsum*—defence of the Christian faith against paganism.

4) *Exhortation to Martyrdom.*

Origen sees degrees of spiritual life in the Sapiential Books [with] Proverbs, for beginners; Ecclesiastes, for proficients; [and] Canticle of Canticles, for [the] perfect. [His] doctrine of the active and the contemplative comes from Philo, who got it from Plato and Aristotle.

[On the] ascetic or active life—*praxis* [he emphasizes]:

1) Self-knowledge—a theme taken up later by St. Bernard, and based on Canticle of Canticles—this is the first step to perfection.

2) Struggle to renounce the world. As we begin to know our passions (object of self- knowledge) and realize our implication in the perishing world, by reason of passion, we begin the struggle to extricate ourselves. This means renunciation, sacrifice, self-denial. Origen places great emphasis on continency and chastity and is a strong defender of virginity. Life-long asceticism is necessary.

3) Imitation of Christ—the ascetic seeks to be re-formed in the likeness of Christ. This gives the soul stability, security in good, and restores lost union with God by charity. This involves crucifixion with Christ, and sharing in His virtues. Origen bases his asceticism on the fact that man, created in the image and likeness of God, has lost his likeness to Him, but remains the image of God. This likeness has to be recovered by grace and love. St. Bernard took over this doctrine and made it the basis of his teaching.

[On the] contemplative life—*theoria*:

1) When one has become purified by self-denial, crucifixion with Christ, and interior trials, one begins to receive a

higher light of knowledge of Christ, principally by a penetration of the spiritual meaning of Scripture. But preparation by interior suffering in union with Christ is essential. This is the characteristic feature of Origen's mysticism; here we find a blending of Neoplatonism and Christianity, intellectualism and sacramentalism.

2) The perfect man is the spiritual man, *pneumatikos*, moved by the Spirit: "He who carries the image of things celestial according to the inner man is led by celestial desires and celestial love." The *pneumatikos* is guided by the Spirit of love. "The soul is moved by this love when having seen the beauty of the Word of God she loves His splendor and receives from Him the arrow and the wound of love" (*In Cantica*, Prologue).

3) The soul aspires to mystical union with the Word of God. She cannot be satisfied with a mediate knowledge of God through human ideas or even through Scriptural symbols: "When the mind is filled with divine knowledge and understanding through no agency of man or angel, then may the mind believe that it receives the very kisses of the Word of God. Therefore the soul prays: Let Him kiss me with the kiss of His mouth" (*In Cantica*). Origen also introduces the idea of "the wound of love" which is developed in Christian mystical tradition. In the Oriental Church, a mystic is referred to as "a man kissed by God." This idea of union with the Logos through union in love and suffering with Christ, the Word Incarnate, is the most fundamental idea in all Christian mystical theology.

4) But normally, the life of the soul seeking Christ is a constant search with alternations of light and darkness, presence and absence. "Frequently I have seen the Spouse pay me a visit and remain often with me. Then He withdrew suddenly and I could not find Him for whom I was looking. That is why I again long for His visit" (*In Cantica*).

5) It is necessary to have discernment to recognize the comings and goings of the Spouse, and to distinguish temptations and false lights among the true lights that come from God. As we grow in experience, we develop the use of the spiritual senses which give us a kind of experience of ineffable and divine realities, "sight for contemplating supracorporal objects, hearing, capable of distinguishing voices which do not sound in the air; . . . smell which perceives that which led Paul to speak of the good odor of Christ; touch which St. John possessed when he laid his hands upon the Word of Life" (*Contra Celsum*, I:48). The spiritual senses do not develop unless we mortify the carnal senses.

6) With the development of the spiritual life, one ascends to the "embrace" of the Word, to "divine inebriation," and to ecstasy (which does not imply a state of alienation from sense, but a transport of spiritual joy and wonder). But it does imply subjection to the power of the Holy Spirit.

7) The summit: union, "mingling of the soul with the Word."

In summary, whatever may be said for or against Origen, he is the most powerful influence on all subsequent mysticism, East and West, particularly West. We find Origen in Cassian, in St. Bernard, St. John of the Cross, the Rhenish mystics, etc. He is practically the source (after the New Testament itself) of Christian mystical thought.

St. Anthony of the Desert

gyptian and Palestinian monasticism arose in the desert, when the *ascetes* (and even some of the virgins) decided that it was necessary for them to withdraw still further from the world. What prompted this movement to the deserts?

It grew in force when the Church became worldly, but began before that. [The year] 313—the Edict of Milan—is an important date in early Church history. Constantine, "converted" (but not baptized) in 312, recognized Christianity and gave it freedom and a place in society. From then on the emperors themselves were to be at least exteriorly Christians. As St. Jerome said, summing up the idea common to Christians of his time and to later tradition: "When the Church came to the princes of the world, she grew in power and wealth but diminished in virtue." Conversions became more numerous but less fervent. The level of Christian life sank and there was more of a tendency for the Christian to become hardly different from his pagan neighbor.

Those seeking the perfect Christian life of renunciation were thus placed in difficulties. First, stricter rules and a more systematic way of asceticism were enjoined upon the ascetes. For instance, virgins were formally bound to stay at home, unless real necessity called them outside (beginnings of enclosure). The hours of the office, Tierce, Sext and None, became customary everywhere, with of course the night office (*anastasis*). Year-round fasting was prescribed. Ascetics began to live in communities—in towns or near them, just outside. However, this was not enough. Visitors disturbed them; the town was near. There were many distractions and temptations. Yet we must not think that they went into the desert expecting to avoid temptation.

The desert was a place of deeper and more spiritual temptation, not just a refuge from the world. What led them to the desert? The examples of St. John Baptist, Elias, and above all of Christ Himself. The ideal was one of silence, solitude, dependence on God. Direct dependence on God is the vocation of the solitary. Perfect abandonment is proper to the monastic state, because it is a literal and exact fulfillment of the Gospel.

Enter St. Anthony

St. Anthony of the Desert was the classic example of a monastic conversion, and the life of Anthony, written by St. Athanasius for some Western monks between 356 and 357, is the most important monument of tradition on the monastic origins. It should be read by all monks. In the *Life of St. Anthony* we find all the essential elements of the early monastic ideal.

The idea that vocations to the desert came with the Edict of Constantine is not quite accurate. There were already many hermits in the desert before that. St. Anthony embraced the hermit life about 270, and went into the desert at Pispir about 285. He had gathered many disciples around him before 313.

He was born at Coma, Middle Egypt, about 251. At the very first, Anthony had ascetic inclinations. He wanted like Jacob "to dwell a plain man in his house" (Gen. 25:27)—avoided the company of other children. He was simple and obedient, loved church services, and listened carefully to the Word of God when it was read—this is important, because here he got his vocation.

[In] 270, [after] meditating on the vocation of the Apostles who left all to follow Christ, and on the renunciation of the first Christians, entering church, he hears read the classical passage from Matthew 19, that of the vocation offered the rich young man: "If thou wilt be perfect, go, sell what thou hast, and give to the poor, and thou shalt have treasure in heaven; and come follow me." (Mt. 19:21) Anthony took this as addressed to himself, and immediately went out, sold all he had, gave to the poor and to his sister. Later, hearing another precept of Christ in the Gospel, "Do not be anxious about tomorrow" (Matt. 6:34), he takes a further step, places his sister (of whom he had care) in a convent; he becomes an ascete outside his home village.

In the first stages of his ascetic life, he works with his hands, seeks out models of virtue in the other ascetes, prays constantly, pays close attention to the reading of Sacred Scripture. He did not know how to read himself, but remembered long passages of Scripture by heart, "his memory serving him instead of books."

[Then came his] first temptations. The Enemy is soon on the scene, and strives to break Anthony's resolution with temptations. Their order is significant. First: anxiety about property, his sister, food; worry about weakness of body and his ability to persevere. Second: violent temptations of the flesh. Anthony replies by meditation—on what? "He extinguished the illusion by meditating on Christ and reflecting on the nobility that is ours through Christ, and on the spiritual nature of the soul." Note the positive and optimistic basis of monastic asceticism— the Incarnation has raised us to the level of sons of God, highest nobility. Our aim should be to live up to this. Third: pride. The devil flatters him, tries to make him take pride in the fact that he is a "great ascetic" and "not like other men." Anthony condemns him. The Savior triumphs in Anthony.

Anthony consolidated his gains by discretion, studying the manifold wiles of the enemy, and by self-discipline. Showing great fervor and zeal, he is able to practice extraordinary mortifications, passing nights without sleep and eating only bread and water. He goes out to the tombs, near the town and lives as a recluse in a tomb. Here is a new phase of struggle. The devils beat him and leave him for dead. He is taken back for burial to his village church, but gets up at midnight and returns to the tombs. The temptations are renewed; the devil tries to terrify him. The Lord appears, and declares that He had waited to see Anthony's struggle.

Anthony, after this "novitiate," starts out for the desert. He lives as a recluse in an ancient fort—struggling with the demons. He spent twenty years in this fort and becomes a perfect ascetic and monk (*megaloschemos*). He has reached *apatheia*: "The temper of his soul, too, was faultless, for it was neither straitened as if from grief, nor dissipated by pleasure, nor was it strained by laughter or melancholy. He was not disturbed when he saw the crowd, nor elated at being welcomed by such numbers; he was perfectly calm, as befits a man who is guided by reason and who has remained in his natural state." Anthony has recovered the state in which man was created in Paradise, for which he was intended by God.

As a proof of his *apatheia*, he is unharmed by ferocious animals; for instance, he crosses a canal infested with crocodiles, unharmed, with the aid of prayer. Also, at this point numerous disciples join themselves to him. We mention these points not as biographical data alone, but because of their importance in theological tradition. See also the life of St. Benedict by St. Gregory. When Benedict reaches ascetic perfection and becomes a contemplative, souls are also brought to him to be formed.

The Doctrine of Anthony

Chapter 16 [of Athanasius's *Life of St. Anthony*] begins a sequence of chapters containing Anthony's doctrine. It is presented as a discourse somewhat like the Lord's Sermon on the Mount at the beginning of His public ministry. Here is the essence of his teaching:

1) Scripture and tradition. The scriptures are in themselves sufficient but also there is their relationship with their elder (Anthony) in which they tell him their difficulties

and he relates to them what he knows on the point from his own experience and from the accumulated experience of the ages.

2) Zeal and energy—determination to grow in ascetic perfection in this life in order to reign with God in eternity—the triviality of trial in time, compared with the eternal reward. Corollary to this are poverty: renounce possessions in this life; seek rather to gain virtues (treasure in heaven); constancy: sustained efforts, not giving up—avoid neglect; need of watchfulness; "synergy": the Lord works with those who give themselves generously to ascetic effort (the Pelagian controversy in the West would lead to clarifications in this matter); charity and daily thought of death, so that we forgive others at all times; the thought of hell: its power in dispelling carnal temptation. "Perfection is within our reach."

3) The goodness of the soul in its natural state. Here we come to an important argument, the foundation stone on which his asceticism is built. God created the soul beautiful and upright in His own image. This beauty is its natural state. To be perfect, we have only to be as God created us, that is to say we have only to "live according to our (true) nature." This sounds exactly the opposite to what we read in ascetic treatises today: that sin consists in following nature, and virtue in going against nature. Modern writers consider nature in its fallen condition; Anthony and the Fathers (up to Augustine, who is pessimistic) consider nature in its original integrity. "If . . . perfection were a thing to be acquired from without, it would indeed be difficult; but, since it is within us, let us guard against our evil thoughts and let us constantly keep our soul for the Lord, as a trust reserved from Him . . . so that He may recognize His work as being the same as when He made it."

4) Demonology [through] special vices. Two great groups, "anger" (irascible passions) and concupiscence (desires for gratification). These passions are incited within us by demons, and they are various "spirits" against which we must guard with constant watchfulness. (This reappears as the essence of Cassian, as we shall see.) These demons are not absolutely evil in themselves; they were created by God and all creatures of God are good. But they envy men and try to prevent them from rising to heaven whence the demons fell. We need the gift of discernment of spirits to detect their wiles. The tactics of the demons are evil thoughts; phantasms; false visions and prophecies; terrifying visions. They use extraordinary and spectacular means, but they also use subtle and less obvious means—for instance: urging to indiscreet fasts and prayers (breaking our sleep); trying to cause despair at our past sins; causing *acedia* and disgust; quoting the scriptures vainly. He warns especially against the prophecies and specious visions they bring to ascetics. This should all be regarded as a temptation; we should serve God not for extraordinary powers, but for love of Him. This doctrine is that of St. John of the Cross (*Ascent of Mount Carmel*, especially book two).

The Later Life of Anthony

He seeks martyrdom in Alexandria, but in vain. His reputation for miracles brings crowds to him. So he retires to Pispir. There follows a further exposition of his doctrine at Pispir. The later teaching of St. Anthony is more mild—with an emphasis on controlling anger, and on what resembles examination of conscience:

> Let us note and write down our deeds and the movements of our soul as if we were to tell them to each other. . . .
> [I]f we write our thoughts as if to tell them to one another, we shall guard ourselves the better from foul thoughts through shame of having them known.

Hence there is some justification for keeping a journal if even St. Anthony recommended the practice! But it must be objective.

His virtues and his miracles are emphasized, his orthodoxy especially. He makes a wise apologia against paganism (these chapters probably reflect the doctrine of St. Athanasius as much as that of Anthony). His prediction of Arianism and his death bring the work to a close. This *Life* is a great document of monastic tradition, perhaps the very greatest, second to no other, even to the *Rule* of St. Benedict. It is one of the great sources of Eastern and Western monasticism, and shows the monk as a soldier of Christ, a man of God, and a man of the Church.

St. Pachomius and the Cenobites

With St. Anthony we have seen the beginning of monasticism in its purest and most primitive form: that of the anchorites. These had a species of community life, in the sense that there were groups of hermits living in certain regions and coming together at times for Mass. Of these some lived altogether by themselves, some lived two or three in a cell. But their life was not organized, and was not meant to be organized.

Cenobites vs. Hermits

With Pachomius, we find organized community life. And here begins an old debate: between cenobites and hermits. It was to last a long time, and the thread of argument runs all through the Desert Fathers' literature. Some are for the free, unorganized life of the hermit living alone with God. Others are for the safer, more consistent, organized life of communities. The argument sometimes gets quite heated, and in the end the cenobites, for all practical purposes, won out. The eremitical ideal remains still the highest ideal of monasticism, especially in the Orient. But in practice cenobitism is what is advocated. Rarely, from time to time, in monastic tradition, the hermit life reappears. It is something that is always there and must always be there but it will remain a special vocation. The life of the cenobite is the "ordinary" and "normal" monastic way.

St. Basil visited Egypt and returned with a strong bias in favor of the cenobites and against the hermits. Reasons: the cenobite is sanctified more easily and more surely by obedience and charity, Gospel virtues. The hermit life is more subject to dangerous illusions. St. Basil manifests real bias on these points. He does not give the hermits a fair hearing. Perhaps he had witnessed too many abuses in Egypt. The *Verba Seniorum* on the other hand bear witness to the beauty and simplicity of the eremitical way. St. Benedict followed St. Basil in preferring the cenobitic life for monks as a whole. He does not exclude hermits, but they are the exception, and need long preparation in the cenobium. St. Theodore Studite in the East, strongly emphasized cenobitism at the monastery of Studion, Constantinople. Cîteaux and Cluny were both strongly cenobitical, yet note that both allowed exceptional vocations to live in solitude. This however was rare. Note: St. Romuald, St. Bruno (Camaldolese and Carthusians) bring a renewal of emphasis on hermit life in the west (11th century). There were always and everywhere men living as hermits in the middle ages—also recluses.

St. Pachomius's Life Briefly

In 292, Pachomius was born of pagan parents in Upper Egypt. [In] 313–314, in the army of Constantine, edified by [the] charity of Christians to prisoners, after discharge he becomes a Christian. A vision shows him the way to the cenobitic life, a life of "sweetness" filling the whole earth. [In] 317, however, Pachomius first begins to lead a traditional hermit life, under the guidance of Abbot Palemon. He spends four years as a hermit and receives a second vision like the first: the cenobitic life represented as honey covering the earth. [By] 324, after his third and fourth visions, he establishes the cenobium at Tabenna. [In] 346, [we see the] death of St. Pachomius.

The Rule of Pachomius

A Latin digest of the Rule of St. Pachomius has come down to us from the hand of St. Jerome. It is especially interesting because in it we recognize not only the broad general outline of the cenobitic life as we know it, but also many familiar details of monastic regularity. Here we come face-to-face with the familiar structure of monasticism as an institution.

The monastery is a large community subdivided into smaller groups. Pachomian monasticism was built on a military plan. The various groups are under the command of subordinate officers, responsible to superior officers. Each group is responsible for a certain share in the monastic work, or liturgy. They take turns in furnishing certain goods or services. The monastery is surrounded by an enclosure from which women are excluded. Monks cannot go out without permission. The head of the whole monastery is the *higumenos*. Under him are the houses presided over by chiefs, forty in a house. The houses are divided into squads of twenty under a lieutenant. There are about thirty or forty houses in a monastery (i.e., about 1,500 monks). The houses are charged with certain jobs, or trades. Hence the members of each house generally do the same work and carry on the same trade. They also take turns weekly in fulfilling community services—providing cooks, etc. Seniority in fulfilling communal offices is determined by the time of entrance into the monastery, as in St. Benedict.

The material side of the life [is] work and poverty. Strict common life was prescribed for the Egyptian cenobites. Articles of clothing were issued from the common store; each was allowed a mat to sleep on, clothes, and nothing more. No one was allowed to keep food in his cell or to bring food there with him when he returned from infirmary. No one could cook on his own or build a fire on his own. All such things were in common. No wine was allowed except to the sick. Food was cooked and distributed from a common kitchen and, except on great occasions, was picked up there and eaten in the *domus*. No one could pick fruits or vegetables from [the] garden on his own. Cooks were not to prepare anything for themselves that was beyond the common rations. No closed cells were allowed, but apparently each had his own cell. It was even decreed that tweezers for taking thorns out of bare feet could not be had except in common, and were to hang in the window where the books were kept.

The business of the monastery was strictly and efficiently regulated. Each week the *domus* had to furnish an account of production to the *higumenos*. Materials and tools were distributed at a central point and work was done in the *domus*. Tools were kept for a week, and redistributed at the end of the week. Work was distributed every evening for the following day. There was an annual shakeup in the distribution of jobs. Not only were the jobs redistributed, and the officers changed, but also sins and public penances were remitted, and monks were supposed also to make up all quarrels and start afresh from scratch.

Regularity: Whereas for the hermit the great thing is individual generosity in prayer, solitude, compunction and penance, for the cenobite external regularity becomes very important. The life is built on it. Prayer life is integrated in the regular exercises. Trumpets announce the hours of prayer. As soon as the trumpet sounds, the monk drops everything and praying mentally (this is insisted on), starts for the place of prayer. Great emphasis is placed on punctuality, on doing everything together and in order. The Pachomian monastery had an air of strict military discipline.

Penances: A regular system of penances protected the framework of regularity, penances for tardiness, for losing things, etc. (One had to go three days without the lost article before it was replaced.) Those who were late had to stand in a place apart. If one left garments out on the line to dry for three days, he was penanced. Penance was prescribed for one who did not imme-diately make known the flight of one of the brethren. Laziness and idleness were severely reproved. The monk had to keep occupied with work or prayer or both. There were severe pen-ances for taking objects assigned to others, or from the common store.

Prompt and universal obedience were emphasized at all times. Independent activities were reproved, even in the smallest things. There were severe reprimands for those who argued with superiors. The monk should not presume to go out in a boat without permission, to cut his hair or that of another unless appointed for the job, to work on his own, etc. Yet at the same time there was much room for individuality in the spiritual life. The spiritual life was not strictly regimented. Individuals could arrange their meals according to inspirations of grace, fast more or less as their conscience dictated (with approval of a direc-tor)—some ate at None, some ate in the evening only, etc. This was easy since there was not much cooked food, and most ate only bread and raw vegetables, olives, fruits. Nothing was to be preferred to the work of God.

Community life: silence was insisted upon—also a certain recollection and solitude. The monks were discouraged from being intimate with one another, and were told to keep to them-selves (had to stay always one cubit apart at least, and not go for walks together). There were disputations (conferences) twice a week by [the] *Praepositus*[1] [and] penances for sleeping at them. The monks discussed among themselves what was said at them. Great emphasis is placed on charity and meekness in community and there is much legislation to curb disobedient, rebellious, or discontented monks. Even those who sit around with sour ex-pressions are admonished.

---

[1] Superior of the local monastery. The connotation in Latin is most like "commander," also military.

Guests: There was a certain latitude in visiting one's relatives or being visited by them. One could go home for special occasions, with a companion. One received visitors also with a companion (as in orders of nuns today). One could eat food brought by guests, but when they left, the extra food had to be turned in for the sick. Clerical visitors came to choir with the monks.

Novices: The formation of the new monks was given special care. We can see [in Pachomius] the sources of St. Benedict's chapter on the reception of novices. They were to be kept waiting at the gate a few days: a postulancy in which they are taught the Our Father and a few psalms. His motives are tested to see whether he is entering out of fear of punishment for crime or for some other trouble, whether he can really renounce his family and possessions, and if he is potentially a man of prayer. As part of his formation the postulant is taught to read and write, and it is prescribed that he have classes at Prime, Tierce, and Sext if necessary:

> Also, one unwilling to read will be compelled to do so, and there will be no one at all within the monastery who has not learned his letters and memorized some of the scriptures.

It is said that they had to know by heart the Psalms and the New Testament before fully becoming monks. When it is decided that he is good material, he is taught the other rules and observances at the gate, still. And this preparation (novitiate) goes on for some time. Finally, the gatekeeper brings him in to the community, he is stripped of secular clothes and vested in monastic habit and joins the monks.

The detailed picture of Pachomian cenobitism may seem a little fearsome. It is misleading, seen only from the outside.

The spirit of St. Pachomius was not simply one of military efficiency, but of deep Christian charity. Charity was first and foremost in the cenobitic life. However, when one legislated for such a big monastic organization, and created such a complex system for the monks, there was always grave danger of it becoming a machine, a big business, or an army outfit. The danger for hermits is individualism and anarchy. The danger for cenobites is excessive organisation, totalitarianism, and mechanical routine. In either case, the only remedy is fidelity to grace, close union with the Holy Spirit Who breathes the divine life into souls and informs rules and regulations with the "breath of life" without which they are only empty forms. This is the hermit's own responsibility. In the cenobium, the responsibility rests first of all with superiors, but the subject too must be careful not to let himself become merely a passive cog in a machine. A monastery must be an organism, not just an organization.

St. Basil of Caesarea

S t. Basil came to Egypt as a critic of the anchorites and a reformer of the cenobitic life.

His Life Briefly

Basil was born about 329 in Caesarea, Cappadocia. His family was Christian and ascetic. His elder sister Macrina had a vow of virginity; she took part in his education. Later his mother and Macrina retired to country property of theirs called Annesi on the banks of the Iris and began to live the monastic life together with other virgins, and with his younger brother Peter, who acted as [a] kind of cellarer. In 351, at the same time as his sister retired to solitude, Basil went to Athens to study. There he met Gregory Nazianzen, and spoke to him of monastic life. His other brother retired to solitude in 352. Basil travelled to Alexandria, Egypt, Palestine and saw monastic life at first hand. In 358, returning from studies and travels, Basil sells all his goods and retires to [the] banks of the Iris at Annesi to live as a monk. He is joined by Gregory Nazianzen. In 364 he writes *Rules*, or begins the redaction of them. He kept returning to this work and revising throughout his life. In 365 he was called to Caesarea by Bishop Eusebius, to aid him in the chancery and was ordained priest. In 370, Basil becomes Bishop of Caesarea. He continued ascetic life—longed for monastery—and founded a hospital at Caesarea which he confided to monks (monks in active life now): a "city of charity."

As bishop, Basil struggled for peace of the Church against Arianism. Athanasius was a Church politician, Basil primarily a theologian. He was in the Nicene-Origenist tradition.[1] He hates controversy, strives to bring [the] Church back to simplicity of faith, [and] defends the divinity of [the] Holy Spirit. His theology is oriented to contemplation as much as it is to dogmatic controversy:

> Basil's true greatness becomes apparent only when he is studied in the context of the conflicts of his age and his role is properly understood. As an ecclesiastical politician Basil did not display the rocklike strength of Athanasius; as a theologian he did not possess the harmony and universality of his younger brother, Gregory of Nyssa; as a monk he did not possess the subtle refinement of some of the later mystics. But these things must not be interpreted as moral weaknesses. On the contrary, it was his very devotion to the needs of the hour which compelled him constantly to vary his tactics and made it impossible for him to develop his rich talents in peace. He found his work as an ecclesiastical politician so difficult because he was not only wiser and more far-seeing but also more profound and more honest than most of his colleagues. It is thanks to him in the first place that the State Church of the Nicenes, which had been built so quickly, not only celebrated easy victories but retained a real theological life and intellectual freedom.[2]

(The same can be said of St. Athanasius, but to a lesser degree.) In 379, St. Basil [died].

---

[1] The "Origenist Controversy" will be alluded to many times in these lectures until Lecture 13 where Merton discusses it fully.

[2] Hans Von Campenhausen, *The Fathers of the Greek Church*, trans. Stanley Godman (New York: Pantheon, 1959), 91–92.

The Writings of St. Basil

[Basil's writings are] Dogmatic: *Adversus Eunomium*; *Homilies on Creation* etc.; *De Spiritu Sancto*; *De Baptismo*. [As with] St. Gregory of Nyssa, we must *not* separate theology and spirituality in the Greek Fathers.

. [They are also] Ascetic and Monastic, generally grouped together as the *Asceticon*, or *Opera Ascetica*, books on the following subjects: The Renunciation of the World; Ascetic Discipline; Judgement, and Faith; Letters; and above all the *Rules*: *The Long Rules: Regulae Fusius Tractatae*, a kind of spiritual directory for the monastic life; *The Short Rules: Regulae Brevius Tractatae*, a catechetical series of solutions to cases and problems in the monastic life. (The collection called *Ascetical Works* of St. Basil in English, in the Fathers of the Church series, contains most of the above [not the *Short Rules*] and also some homilies on the ascetic life which are very good.)[3]

[Major topics:]

1) *Doctrine on perfection*—All Christians are called to perfection and sanctity, by consecration to God and by faithfully carrying out His holy will. But monks above all have given themselves completely to the pursuit of perfection, to seeking God. The characteristic of St. Basil's doctrine of monastic perfection is that he seeks to be more prudent and discreet than the Fathers of Egypt, to avoid their exaggerations, and to lead all, or at least greater numbers, more safely to God in a wisely regulated monastic life.

   Monks act in the interests of charity above all, since perfection consists in charity. Like St. Bernard in *De Diligendo Deo*, St. Basil gives some of the reasons for loving God. Monastic life is built on gratitude for God's love. The

---

[3] St. Basil, *Ascetical Works*, trans. Sister M. Monica Wagner, CSC, Fathers of the Church, vol. 9 (Washington, DC: Catholic University of America Press, 1950).

monastic family life in which the elders are full of fatherly or brotherly concern for the juniors, is the supreme means to perfection in charity. Emphasis is placed on obedience, docility, and humility as the characteristic monastic virtues. But poverty and austerity remain absolutely essential.

2) *Prayer is the first duty of the monk*—Of very great importance is self-custody and guarding against distraction: "As each kind of mastery demands its own specific and appropriate training, so the discipline for pleasing God in accordance with the Gospel of Christ is practiced by detaching oneself from the cares of the world and by complete withdrawal from its distractions." The purpose of the life of prayer is not only to glorify God but also to lead the soul to perfect union with Him. However St. Basil speaks little of contemplation. He is primarily an active soul, and his brother Gregory of Nyssa is the contemplative of the family. Note that in the cenobitic tradition the keynote has been given by active, ascetic, organizing, administrating saints like Basil rather than by interior and contemplative saints like Gregory of Nyssa. These appeal more to solitaries.

3) *Spiritual progress*—St. Basil does not admit of a spiritual life in which everything is static. One does not fly to the monastery and then remain in the same state for the rest of his life. We must *grow* in perfection.

The monk lives face to face with the truth that sin is the great obstacle between himself and God. Hence his life is first of all a combat against sin, a struggle for liberation from all sin. The only evil is that which depends on our own power. "Evil" which comes from outside ourselves can be turned to good. But sin, which comes from within us, always harms us, is always a true evil. In his teaching on liberation from sin St. Basil resembles and follows the Stoics.

The starting point in the spiritual ascent is self-knowledge and self-custody: "If, then, we would safely traverse the road of life lying before us, and offer to Christ our body and soul alike free from the shame of wounds, and receive the crown for this victory, we must always and everywhere keep the eyes of our soul wide open, holding in suspicion everything that gives pleasure. We must unhesitatingly pass by such things, without allowing our thoughts to rest in them."

Then comes resolute entrance into the spiritual combat, the struggle against passion and self-love. St. Basil analyzes the various vices and describes the action of the virtues that oppose them. The early monks were psychologists and observers of human nature. The most important of the virtues is humility because by it we return to our original state. Our natural state is that of sons of God, men made in the image and likeness of God. Humility restores us to our complete dependence on God from whom we have received, and must yet receive, all that we are and all that we have.

The notion of the three divisions of the spiritual life: purgative, illuminative and unitive, is present in St. Basil, but not emphasized.

4) *Union with God*—is the summit of the spiritual life because he who is fully united to God, and resembles Him most perfectly, gives Him the greatest glory. This means the intellect is filled with God's truth. And one is able to share that truth with others. The will is filled with His love which unites us closely to God so that no suffering can separate us from Him.

Basilian Cenobitism

Pachomian monasticism was organized, but the spirit remained more individualistic. The Pachomian monastery was not a family, or a real community, but a collection of small groups, cemented together by organization and discipline. St. Basil emphasizes [by contrast] the social and communal heart of the cenobitic life.

The value of the cenobitic life is not to be sought in organization but in love—something deeper and more interior. The monastic community is a family, a body, and the members share in the life and activities of the body. The good of one is the good of all. No one seeks his own good in the monastic community. Each is for all and all are for each. Each helps the other, and in helping others helps himself. Each makes up for what the other lacks. No one has to be complete and self-sufficient; what he has not, another will supply. Nothing is wasted in the monastic life— even spiritually. One who is weak and poor, can still contribute whatever small talent he has, and go on, supported by the others. Thus, the perfect life is accessible to all. The good things of God are easily shared in community, and the sharing increases them. The cenobitic life offers greater protection against the devil. The variety of duties offers scope for various talents and graces— some can take care of guests, of the sick, etc., others are free to devote themselves more exclusively to prayer. In the monastery, there is always the power of living example. The good of the community is the divine will.

Hence in community life the divine will is easy to know and follow. The great enemy is self-will. Everything else in the monastery can be consecrated to God, but not this.

Other Cappadocian Fathers: The Two Gregories

We ought to pause at least long enough to make the acquaintance of two great monastic theologians, friends and confreres of St. Basil. One of them, Gregory of Nyssa, is the saint's blood brother. The other is his close friend.

St. Gregory Nazianzen

Gregory was born about 330. He studied with St. Basil in Athens and had also studied at Caesarea (where Origen had taught) and Alexandria—hence an Origenist. In 359 he became a monk with Basil, on the banks of the Iris. He devoted himself to asceticism and study and composed the *Philocalia*, an anthology of the best passages from Origen (not to be confused with another *Philocalia*: Orthodox texts on prayer).[1] In 362, he is reluctantly ordained priest but afterwards returns to solitude, but was recalled to active life and supported orthodoxy in the

---

[1] Most of all, not to be confused by the spelling of the title word. This work is known to readers in English as *The Philokalia: The Complete Text*, compiled by St. Nikodemos of the Holy Mountain and St. Makarios of Corinth, trans. and ed. G. F. H. Palmer, Philip Sherrard, and Kallistos Ware, 4 volumes (London: Faber & Faber, 1979–95).

Arian conflict. In 371, he is reluctantly consecrated bishop of Sasimes by Basil, but afterwards regrets it and flees once again to solitude; he enjoyed contemplative life for a while in the monastery of St. Thecla at Selucia. In 379, he consents to take over the Diocese of Constantinople, overrun with Arians. His center is a small semi-private chapel, where he gives discourses and gradually wins over intellectuals and influential people to orthodoxy. The Arians had established a bishop of their own in the see, but Theodosius supported Gregory and had him enthroned and acclaimed in Sancta Sophia. Gregory was acknowledged by the Eastern Council of Constantinople, 381, but then, opposed by Egyptian and Macedonian bishops who came late, he resigned. In 381–383 he administered the vacant diocese of Nazianz and in 381–389 retired to solitude, and died there.

It is clear from this outline that Gregory did not adapt well to the active and episcopal life. Not that he was not a gifted bishop, but he had no flair for politics. He was a truly spiritual man, and a true contemplative. His simplicity made him unfit for politics. He was sensitive and sincere, hence was greatly hurt by betrayals and insincerities of others. Generous and unselfish, he would not fight for his own interests. Although he preferred the contemplative life, he sacrificed that life several times, sincerely desiring to do what seemed to be the will of God. But he was unable to become a "politician" and returned to solitude. His life is a series of repeated failures in the active world, and repeated returns to contemplation. His chief greatness is as a theologian and preacher, inheriting the mystical tradition of Origen.

His works: *Sermons*, especially those preached at Constantinople in 380, against the Arians; *Poems*, mostly written during the last contemplative period of his life: on moral and dogmatic topics, and one long autobiographical poem *De Vita Sua*; *Letters*, mostly of historical interest. St. Gregory Nazianzen has left us little that is of specific importance for monastic theology and spirituality.

St. Gregory of Nyssa

St. Gregory of Nazianz was a dogmatic theologian and an orator. His writings were more popular in the eighteenth and nineteenth centuries, because they had an apologetic trend. But he is not as useful to monks as St. Gregory of Nyssa, who has come into our own as a great comtemplative theologian especially strong in the monastic tradition. Fr. Daniélou's book *Platonisme et Théologie Mystique*[2] and the French translation of *De Vita Moysis*, both of which appeared during World War II, started a revival of studies and admiration for St. Gregory of Nyssa, as did also the work of Fr. Hans Urs von Balthasar. It can be said that Gregory of Nyssa is one of the most important figures in the contemplative revival of Patristic studies—a significant spiritual movement of our time.

Gregory was born about 330. He was ordained lector while young, but was seduced by the revival of pagan culture under Julian. He became a professor of rhetoric and then married. But exhorted by St. Basil and St. Gregory Nazianzen, he left the world to join them and live as a monk on the banks of the Iris (about 361). After ten years of solitude, he becomes bishop of Nyssa, 371. Gregory was not happy at Nyssa. He was opposed by the emperor, framed and deposed on charge of wasting funds (374) but was restored as bishop in 377. On the death of St. Basil, January 1, 379, Gregory took over his theological and ecclesiastical work, and carried on where Basil had left off. He was involved in all the political struggles of this time. He too was not very adept at politics, but as a theologian he played an important part in the Council of Constantinople (381) and was one of the out-

---

[2] *Platonism and Mystical Theology*, a work not yet translated into English.

standing figures there—[he] gained a reputation as a great preacher in Constantinople. The Council of Constantinople was the triumph of St. Basil's ideas and of those of St. Gregory. After the Council he went to Arabia and Egypt on church business. Returning to Jerusalem he was accused of Apollinarism[3] but goes to Constantinople, in high favor; 380–386 marks the peak of his career. From 387 onward, in retirement, he devotes himself to writing.

Of the three great Cappadocian Fathers, Gregory of Nyssa is the greatest as mystic and spiritual theologian. He is the greatest contemplative of the three, the deepest, most mystical, and most spiritual. His theology is drawn from experience and it is evident that his experience was the deepest of all the Greek Fathers, including St. Maximus and Pseudo-Denys. But besides being a mystic he is also a philosopher, a speculative thinker. This combination makes his work original and significant.

The importance of Gregory of Nyssa is as a source of Christian mystical theology. He transmits the tradition of Origen, purified and deepened by a more spiritual experience, to later theologians like Pseudo-Denys. St. Gregory of Nyssa stands side-by-side with another Origenist and mystic, Evagrius Ponticus (a Desert Father), who is more an intellectual. Gregory gives the primacy to love. The influence of St. Gregory of Nyssa is considerable in the West, and especially on the Cistercian William of St. Thierry, through whom the theology of Gregory of Nyssa became part of the Cistercian heritage.

Gregory of Nyssa's Writings

The dogmatic and controversial writings of St. Gregory of Nyssa are less important. The main one is *Contra Eunomium,*

---

[3] Heresy originating with Apollinaris of Laodicea (d. 390) which held that Jesus had a human body but a divine mind. The Council of Constantinople condemned this view in 381, but it persisted in some quarters.

which carried on controversy begun by St. Basil with the Arian bishop Eunomius. Eunomius held that the essence of God was innascibility, and hence the Son could not be God; also that the essence of God could be clearly known by man: Gregory stands up strongly for the "darkness" which obscures the mind of man in presence of the transcendent mystery of God—this is one of the most important ideas in his mystical theology: to know God "by unknowing." [Then there is] *Contra Apollinarem*—against the Apollinarist heresy that in Christ the Word took the place of the human mind; [and] *Oratio Catechetica*—exposition of dogmas of Trinity, Incarnation, Redemption.

[From the] spiritual writings, first it should be remarked that this distinction between "theological writings" and "spiritual writings" is very misleading in St. Gregory of Nyssa. His spirituality is his theology and his theology is entirely spiritual. Nowadays there is a gulf separating theology (technical dogma and moral) from spirituality (meditations, devotions, psychology of the spiritual life, mysticism and asceticism). For St. Gregory and the Greek Fathers the two are inseparable, and especially for St. Gregory. For example his treatise on the creation of man, *De Hominis Opificio*, is not merely theological and philosophical in the technical sense, but is also a study of man as a creature destined for contemplation. Hence there is spiritual, mystical theology in this work. What we might call more technically theological works of the Greek Fathers are works of controversy with emphasis on special technical points. But we have seen above that even Gregory's *Contra Eunomium* has important implications for the mystical life.

For the Greek Fathers, theology is above all and essentially *mystical* theology, and all learning culminates in true theology, the vision of God. St. Bonaventure above all carries on this tradition in the scholastic era, but scholasticism in general tends to degenerate into technical knowledge *about* God, and tends less and less to lead to contemplation of Him.

The writings:

De Virginitate—His first book, written to aid St. Basil in establishing his monastery. Theme: Christian perfection. The virgin soul is the spouse of Christ. The monastic life is the best means of living a *bios angelikos* (angelic life) and cultivating perfect purity of heart.

Short treatises on perfection, mortification, the Christian life.

A biography of his sister *St. Macrina.*

In Hexameron (379)—A parallel to St. Basil's treatise on the Hexameron. Purpose: To throw new light on the facts exposed by Basil; to show the deep underlying causes and purposes at work in creation.

De Hominis Opificio—About the same time, completes St. Basil's treatise on creation. St. Basil had not taken the sixth day, creation of man. Man is made for contemplation. This treatise had considerable influence on William of St. Thierry. Man is made up of *psyche* (animal nature, body); *nous, mens, ratio* (rational nature, mind); *pneuma, spiritus* (spiritual life, grace, divinization). Perfection is the balance and ordering of all these three: body, mind, and spirit—not just the development of the mind in a purely mental spirituality at the expense of body and spirit. Just as God is beyond all clear knowledge, so the image in us is beyond the clear grasp of our intelligence. Man's job in life is to reproduce in the depths of the soul his divine likeness. This consists in the right use of his freedom, which is his royal dignity and this is entirely summed up in the return to God by pure love.

[On the subject of] spiritual interpretation of Scripture, following Origen and Philo, but going much deeper than either one, Gregory interprets Old Testament books as describing the spiritual ascent of the soul to God. *De Vita Moysis*, one of the greatest mystical works of the Greek Fathers, is divided into two parts: 1) *Historia*—the literal sense, but not scientific; emphasis is moral and hortatory, really a kind of saint's life, rather than a scriptural study. Remember that for the early Fathers, the "saints" were for the most part the saints of the Old Testament (except for the martyrs). Here he follows Philo closely, often word for word. 2) *Theoria*—the mystical interpretation. Especially notable is the idea that Moses' ascent of the mountain into the cloud symbolizes contact of the soul with the transcendent "darkness" of God. This is the mysticism of "night"—of darkness (apophatic mysticism) which forms one important tradition in Christian mystical theology contrasted with the mystics of "light" (cataphatic) in another tradition.

The most important mystics of darkness: St. Gregory of Nyssa, Pseudo-Dionysius, St. John of the Cross, Eckhart. Mystics of light: Origen, St. Bernard, St. Teresa of Avila etc. The latter are the more common. St. Gregory says (concerning Exodus 19):

> Religious knowledge starts out as light (the burning bush) when it first appears: for then it is opposed to impiety, which is darkness, and this darkness is scattered by joy in the light. But the more the spirit, in its forward progress attains, by a greater and more perfect application, to the understanding of the realities and comes closer to contemplation, the more it realizes that the divine nature is invisible. Having left behind all appearances, not only those perceived by the senses but also those which the intelligence believes itself to see, the spirit enters more and more into the interior until it penetrates, by its striving, even unto the Invisible and the Unknowable, and there it sees God. The true knowledge of Him that it seeks and the true vision of Him consists in seeing that He is invisible, because He transcends all knowledge, and is hidden on all sides by His incomprehensibility as by shadows. (*De Vita Moysis*)

Other Scriptural exegesis:

On the Psalms: Here he finds other material on the ascent to perfection. *On Ecclesiastes*: The illuminative way—subtle and rich discussion of the disillusionment of the soul with material and temporal things, as it ascends to God. Man seeks distraction. He vainly hopes to forget his troubles not so much in enjoying pleasures or acquiring wealth, as in the pursuit of these things. It is the pursuit, the expectation, that gives joy. Hence man lives more and more outside himself and "beyond" himself, and his life becomes a race, a running away from the present into the future, perpetual motion. This is the vanity of Ecclesiastes. The first step to stability is then to be content with what we have and with what we are.

On the Canticle of Canticles: Follows the commentary on Ecclesiastes and completes it, going on to the unitive life. It also adds to mystical theology of Origen's commentary on Canticles, carries it further. It was a more influential work than Origen's, deeper—describes in some detail the gradual approach to Union—the steps by which the Word makes Himself known to the soul as a faint "perfume," as a voice, and finally as food for the soul that is "tasted" and sweet. Finally it describes burning love of God which is proper to union and renders the soul impatient of all that separates it from God—themes that reappear in St. John of the Cross, *Living Flame of Love*.

Two New Testament treatises: *On the Lord's Prayer* stresses the idea of sonship and *parrhesia* (freedom and spontaneity of speech with God) implied by the prayer—man's vocation to help God establish His Kingdom on earth, in souls, by driving out sin. *On the Beatitudes*—one of many Patristic commentaries on the eight Beatitudes (Matthew 5) which treats them as an ascent to mystical perfection, with special emphasis on the sixth ("Blessed are the pure in heart") as referring to contemplation. Here we meet the familiar Patristic doctrine—the soul made in the image of God. The image has been obscured by sin. It must be restored to its perfection by love, then God will again be perfectly mirrored and experienced in the mirror of the soul:

> For the Godhead is purity, freedom from passion, and separation from all evil. If therefore these things be in you, God is indeed in you. Hence, if your thought is without any alloy of evil, free from passion, and alien from all stain, you are

blessed because you are clear of sight. You are able to perceive what is invisible to those who are not purified, because
you have been cleansed; the darkness caused by material
entanglements has been removed from the eyes of your
soul, and so you see the blessed vision radiant in the pure
heaven of your heart. But what is this vision? It is purity,
sanctity, simplicity, and other such luminous reflections of
the Divine Nature, in which God is contemplated.[4]

The great problem is the purification of the heart—this is treated
at length in the sermon.

St. Gregory also wrote three lives, less important for biographical data than for remarks on spirituality: St. Basil, his
brother; St. Macrina, his sister; St. Gregory the Wonderworker
(because he was a disciple of Origen).

For all the various reasons expressed above, St. Gregory of
Nyssa is the most important and most interesting of the Cappadocian Fathers, at least for contemplatives. He requires to be
studied more deeply, however. Perhaps the moment has not yet
come when he is accessible to the average monk with ease—at
least not in English. He may perhaps remain difficult and inaccessible to most.

[4] St. Gregory of Nyssa, *The Lord's Prayer; The Beatitudes*, trans. Hilda
C. Graef, Ancient Christian Writers, vol. 18 (Westminster, MD: Newman,
1954), 149–50.

Palestinian Monasticism and St. Jerome

bout 390 (about the time Cassian was in Egypt), St. Jerome wrote the life of St. Hilarion. Hilarion, as a founder of Palestinian monasticism and disciple of St. Anthony, is an important if somewhat legendary figure. Jerome presents him as the model monk, the type of Palestinian monasticism.

St. Hilarion was born at Tabatha, near Gaza, in Palestine, of pagan parents. He was sent to study in Alexandria, and there became a Christian. Attracted by the fame of St. Anthony, he went to see him, became a monk, spent several months with him, then returned to Palestine to live the monastic life. He was then fifteen years old. He retired to [a] desert place on the coast, infested with robbers: *contempsit mortem, ut mortem evaderet,* "He scorned death that he might escape death." He embraced a life of strict fasting, labor, solitude and penance, suffered temptations like those of St. Anthony, cut his hair once a year—at Easter, never washed his hairshirt, alleging that cleanliness was useless in one who wore a hairshirt.

His fasts: from [ages] twenty-one to twenty-four, he ate a half-pint of lentils soaked in water once a day; from twenty-four to twenty-seven: ate only dry bread with water and salt; from twenty-seven to thirty-one: ate wild herbs and raw roots; from thirty-one to thirty-five: six ounces of barley bread a day, with a few herbs; from thirty-five to sixty-four: "But perceiving his sight to grow dim, and his body to be subject to an itching, with an unnatural kind of scurf and roughness, he added a little oil to this diet," [wrote Alban] Butler; from sixty-four to eighty: cut down one ounce on the bread, ate only five ounces; and at eighty:

> When he was fourscore years of age there were made for him little weak broths or gruels of flour and herbs, the whole quantity of his meat and drink amounting to the weight of four ounces. Thus he passed his whole life; and he never broke his fast until sunset, not even upon the highest feasts, nor in his greatest sickness. [quoting Alban Butler]

Point of this: [the] essential importance of fasting in the ascetic and contemplative life. Not that everyone is obliged to keep the measure of St. Hilarion, but all must fast according to their measure. Fasting is not something one takes on for a time, hoping to give it up. It is a lifelong part of the monastic vocation, with of course room left for modifications in case of need. But we should not seek them without necessity, or be looking for pretexts to give up fasting. (Note: St. Benedict [later] stresses that obedience is more important than fasting.)[1]

When he was eighteen, robbers came to him and said: What would you do if robbers found you? His reply: "The naked person is not afraid of robbers." You can be killed, they continue. "I could," he said, "I could, and so I am not afraid of robbers because I am ready to die." They were edified and converted. Note—the hermit life involves the facing of every possible danger.

At the age of twenty-two he worked his first miracle which was the cure of a barren woman. After that his life is a catalogue of miracles. He cures men from all over the world, and animals,

---

[1] "The reference is evidently to chapter 49 of the *Rule*, which specifies that during Lent the monks are to submit their regimen of fasting to the approval of the abbot." –Patrick O'Connell

including a mad camel tied and dragged by thirty men! He converted many pagans (note missionary aspect of his hermit life).

From his twenties to his seventies, working miracles everywhere, he became the center of a great attraction and cult. Finally, seeing himself surrounded by many monks and pilgrims at all times, he lived in great sorrow, weeping daily, saying, "I have returned to the world—I am receiving my reward in this present life." In the lives of solitary and monastic saints, apostolate is *charismatic* and is fruitful *because of contradiction.* He had prophetic knowledge of the death of St. Anthony.

Although a crowd of 10,000 pilgrims tried to hold him back, he went into the desert of Egypt with a few monks to see that place where St. Anthony had lived and died. St. Anthony had been buried in a secret place, at his own command, lest his bones be taken away and made a center of pilgrimage. After this, he fled into Sicily, where he was unknown. Avoiding the ports, where he might be recognized by oriental traders, he fled inland and lived as a beggar, bringing firewood to town on his back for a livelihood. He was discovered through an announcement made by the devil in a possessed person, who came and threw himself down to be cured at the hut where Hilarion was living in the hills. The miracles begin again. Hilarion then went to Dalmatia, then to Cyprus. Finally he found a very remote place in some mountains of Cyprus where there were no Christians and lived there in peace five years (cf. Charles de Foucauld). There he died at the age of 80.

[Other Palestinian monastics:]

St. Chariton—From Iconium in Asia Minor. He lived in a cave in the Wadi Pharan north of Jerusalem, from 322 on. Here disciples gathered and a monastery was founded. In 355 he moved on to the other side of Jordan to the mountain where Jesus fasted—another monastery was founded which is still there today (Greek monks). Finally he found an inaccessible cave in the desert of Juda—but a third monastery was founded near it—Deir Suka.

St. Euthymius (d. 473), from Armenia, began as a hermit at Wadi Pharan, near St. Chariton, started a cenobium, then founded famous Laura of St. Euthymius, near Bethany (428); it was transformed into a cenobium after his death.

St. Sabas (439–532), a Cappadocian, formed in cenobium of St. Euthymius, lived as a hermit in the Kedron valley near Jerusalem. Then he organized the great Laura of Mar Saba (478), which still exists today, clinging to the side of a cliff. *St. John Damascene* was a monk here—and here wrote all his books. It has three churches, in which liturgy used to be celebrated in three languages according to three rites: Armenian, Syrian, and Greek. Today about thirty monks—Greek Orthodox—live in cells which are partly caves. The monks of St. Sabas also maintained hospitals. He instituted the *Typikon*—basis of oriental monastic liturgy.

Cyril of Scythopolis—a disciple of St. Sabas, lived in great Laura and composed lives of saints.

John Moschus (6th–7th cent.) was a late compiler of monastic stories and legends—the *Spiritual Meadow*—popular—full of "wonders."

St. Jerome

The most famous monk in Palestine was to be St. Jerome whom we will here treat quite briefly. Although a Desert Father, St. Jerome really falls outside the whole scope of these lectures, as a Father and Doctor of the Church and a translator and commentator on Scripture. His vocation was much vaster and more spectacular than that of a simple Desert Father—the same could of course be said for Sts. Basil, Gregory of Nyssa, etc.

He was born at Stridon, Dalmatia, about 347, the child of Christian parents, but was not baptized until later in life. Meanwhile, during his studies in Rome, he led a somewhat dissolute life. Baptized about 365 (age eighteen), he started living as a monk near Aquilaeia in Italy. Here his association with *Rufinus* began. He moved east (about 374), and lived as a monk in the desert of Chalcis, near Antioch, Syria. This was already a monastic center. He was ordained priest at Antioch about 378. The years 382–385 mark his visit to Rome under Pope Damasus. He now has a great reputation. He served Damasus as secretary. It was under Damasus that Jerome gave himself definitely to work on Scripture. He made himself unpopular in Italy by criticizing lax Christians and tepid clergy. From now on he was definitely to be a fighter, and in every battle of his time. Here he met Paula and Eustochium, whose direction he assumed, and they were led by him to monastic life in Palestine. He went with them to Palestine in 385 when, after the death of Pope Damasus, violent opposition to Jerome was let loose in Rome. Occasion was taken to calumniate St. Jerome and his relations with the noble matrons he had directed at Rome, teaching them to read Scripture in original Greek and Hebrew. St. Paula (d. 404) was mother of St. Eustochium and St. Blaesilla. She became a widow at thirty-four, came under [the] influence of St. Jerome, led a consecrated life, was Abbess of [a] convent founded by him at Bethlehem, where she also conducted a hospital—a remarkable instance of nuns living contemplative life—with notable elements of scholarship and works of mercy.

The monastic life as influenced by the presence and character of St. Jerome takes on a very active and aggressive character, although remaining contemplative. For this reason we have to be careful of taking Jerome as a typical Desert Father. On the whole he is not the best of models for contemplatives. He inspires rather those whose spiritual life is aggressive, ascetical, active, and controversial: but these are often people who stir up monastic orders and cause dissension—though when they are really saints they may accomplish much good.

On arriving in Palestine with Paula, Eustochium, and a bevy of other friends, St. Jerome went for a trip around all the holy places, accompanied by them. He continued on down into Egypt, but did not visit Nitria as he hoped. Heat in Alexandria in 386 (summer) drove them all back north. They settle in Bethlehem: two monasteries, one of women, one of men, both founded by St. Paula. St. Jerome finishes his life here, thirty-five years of very fruitful activity, surrounded by his monks. From 390 to 405 he is engaged in translation of the Bible (Vulgate)—learned Hebrew from rabbis who slipped in to monastery under cover of darkness (and collected a good fee for their lessons). He wrote commentaries on various books of the Bible at this same time, carried on controversies, wrote innumerable letters. Sulpicius Severus described Jerome thus: "He is constantly immersed in study, wholly plunged in his books he gives himself no rest either day or night; he is incessantly occupied in reading or writing" [in his *Dialogues* 1:9].

We shall see later, in discussing Cassian, Jerome's place in the Origenist controversy. Jerome went against Origen, breaking with the Bishop (John) of Jerusalem, who nearly had him thrown out of Palestine, and breaking also with his best friend, Rufinus, who remained faithful to Origen. Jerome, in his *Apology against Rufinus*, accuses the latter of heresy, duplicity etc. Rufinus had followed Jerome to Palestine, a little after the grand tour. He arrived in Palestine with St. Melania the Elder, another ascetic woman of great prominence, [where] he founded a monastery on the Mount of Olives. Like Jerome, Rufinus was a scholar-monk. He translated much of Origen and is important for his (translation) work.

The controversy with Jerome was very unpleasant and was exceptionally hot due to various misunderstandings, Jerome's quick temper and sharp tongue. Rufinus was much more moderate, discreet, and probably the more sensible of the two in this controversy. He made less of an exhibition of violence. The breach was repaired in 397. The controversy is important in monastic history. During the controversy, Rufinus had moved to Italy. Driven out by Visigothic invasion, he died in Sicily where he was with Melania the Younger, in 411.

Other Controversies in the Life of Jerome

Among his very numerous controversies, we enumerate those which have some importance for monastic history.

1) Against *Helvidius* who attacked the virginity of the Blessed Mother (said she had other children after Our Lord). This defence of Our Lady's virginity was also important for consecrated (monastic) virginity.

2) Against *Jovinian* who attacked the life of chastity and continency and preached faith without works. Jerome's defence is important for monastic ascetic doctrine.

3) Against *Vigilantius*, a priest from Spain who had been hospitably received in Jerome's monastery and afterwards wrote a book condemning monastic life and veneration of the saints.

4) Jerome, in collaboration with St. Augustine, helped by Orosius (Augustine's messenger) delved into the *Pelagian* controversy: looked up material on Pelagius for St. Augustine. He joined in the controversy also, and as a result the Pelagians pillaged his monastery. (We shall return to the question of Pelagianism in talking of Cassian).

St. Jerome was especially opposed to the doctrines of *apatheia* (possible freedom from all passion by ascetic works, without grace) and impeccability (the ascetic could by his own efforts, when free from passion, become sinless). There is a phrase in St. Jerome which has a semi-pelagian flavor: *nostrum incipere, illius perficere.* "Our part is to begin [the work of salvation], His is to perfect it." This is certainly stronger than any of the semi-pelagian-seeming phrases in Cassian, yet in Jerome it is always successfully excused, and regarding Cassian, suspicion remains. This is because Cassian was opposed by the strong Augustinian party in the West; Jerome was not. We must be careful to remember that the stigma of heresy or doubtful orthodoxy clings tenaciously sometimes to men who have not taught otherwise than the saints of their time, but have somehow acquired a bad reputation due to "politics."

Jerome's Monastic Doctrine

St. Jerome was a great preacher and apostle of monastic renunciation. His doctrine contains nothing new: what is original in him is the fire and power of exhortation.

Quote from letter fourteen to Heliodorus:

> Why are you a Christian with such a timorous heart? Look at the Apostle Peter quitting his nets; look at the Publican leaving his office for the receipt of custom to become a missionary on the spot. The Son of Man had not where to lay His head, and will you be making use of great doorways and spacious dwellings? If you look for your inheritance in this world, you cannot be the co-heir of Christ. . . . You have promised to be a thorough Christian. . . . But a thorough Christian has nothing but Christ, or if he has anything else he is not perfect. . . . What are you, my brother, doing in the world, you who are greater than the world? . . . Do you dread the poverty of the desert? But Christ says that the poor are blessed. Are you afraid of work? But no athlete wins a prize without toiling hard. Are you thinking of the food you will get here? But if your faith is strong you will not fear being hungry. Are you afraid of bruising your limbs on the bare ground after they have been emaciated by fasting? But the Lord lies down with you on the ground. Do you dread wearing your hair unkempt on your unwashed head? But Christ is your head. Do you shrink from the infinite spaces of the desert? But in your thoughts you will tread the heavens; and whenever you are borne thither in mind you will be no more in the desert. . . . The day will surely come when this corruptible and mortal flesh will put on incorruption and immortality. "Blessed is that servant whom, when his lord shall come, he shall find watching" (Lk. 12:43). On that day when the trumpet shall sound, the nations of the earth shall be smitten with fear, and then you will rejoice!

The monk leaves all to live united with Christ. He has an obligation to do this for, being a member of Christ, he is greater than
the world and should not remain subject to what is beneath him.
He must bravely face the hardships of desert life and deprivation,
trusting in Christ, not in his own power. Finally he must base
his whole monastic life on eschatological hope—the second
coming and the new creation.

Jerome is the first to use *monachus* in Latin. He takes it to
mean "solitary." *Quid facis in turba qui solus es?* "What are you
doing in a crowd, you who are a solitary?" Essentially the monk
is a pilgrim to the promised Land, an exile, following Christ. His
state does not normally allow of the priestly office (which would
mean being in town). He belongs in paradise. "Your homeland
is paradise. Retain your birthright. . . . 'Return to your rest, my
soul' (Ps. 116:7)."

Profession is a second baptism, because [it is] a martydom.
Monastic life is athletic training. Here strength and generosity
are much needed. It is also a militia, under Christ the *Imperator*,
"Emperor." To abandon one's monastic profession is to deny
Christ, like departing from the army.

Monastic life is an angelic life of praise, in proportion as we
sing to God with pure hearts and a record of good works. "Sing
with all your members. Let the hand sing in almsgiving, the foot
sing while going out on a good work." The spiritual and intellectual life of the monk and nun is based on the Bible.

Silence is central. The monk helps the world by weeping in
silence, not by preaching: "not by speaking and discoursing but
by sitting down and keeping quiet." Work is important, at least
the copying of manuscripts. Be slow to write books: "Do not
rush forward quickly to write, and be drawn away from such
trivial nonsense. Spend much time learning what you may teach."

Jerome urged men and women fearlessly to defy the world
and their families in order to renounce worldly life and follow
Christ with courage. This emphasis on courage and dauntless
faith is what makes St. Jerome's letters such necessary reading

for monks and contemplatives (cf. his influence on St. Teresa).[2] Read the classic diatribe in which he urges Heliodorus to trample on his father's prostrate body if the latter lies down across the threshold to prevent him going forth to follow his vocation.

We should all be familiar with these exhortations and meditate on them often. Courage and determination are essential to a real monastic vocation. Without them, we fail to correspond to grace. Pray for determination and fidelity to God's call.

[2] See *The Collected Works of St. Teresa of Avila*, trans. Kieran Kavanaugh, OCD, and Otilio Rodriguez, OCD (Washington, DC: Institute of Carmelite Studies, 1976), 1:40.

The Community of St. Melania

St. Melania

This was the first Latin community of women to be founded in Palestine (373–374). St. Melania, a Roman noble of the *gens Antonia*,[1] a relative of St. Paulinus, lost her husband and two children at the age of twenty-two and decided to leave the world. (One son remains in Rome.) She left for Egypt in 372, visited Nitria, then went to Palestine to get away from Arianism. She founded a convent on the Mount of Olives with a guest house for pilgrims. She died at Jerusalem in 410. A friend of Rufinus, she was attacked, with him, by St. Jerome. Her nuns participated in the liturgical celebrations at the Holy Places.

Important material on St. Melania is found in the *Historia Lausiaca*, written in 419–420, for Palladius was a guest at Melania's convent in 405. Palladius exhibits great praise for Melania and Rufinus: "among men one would not quickly find one who was more understanding, and gracious, and pleasant than he." For twenty-seven years they gave hospitality to pilgrims without charge. They "healed the schism of the Paulinists [monks]." "Now as concerning the possessions of which she stripped herself, and the money which she distributed, being

---

[1] An ancient Roman lineage to which possibly belonged Marcus Antonius (Mark Antony) and many others.

hot as fire with divine zeal, and blazing like flame with the love
of Christ, I alone am not able to recount it, for it belongeth also
unto those who dwell in the country of the Persians to declare
it; for there was no man who was deprived of her alms and gifts,
whether he came from the east, or the west, or the north, or the
south." She returns to Rome to rescue her granddaughter
Melania the Younger from the world and incidentally converts
many others.

She contended with all the women of Senatorial rank and
with all the women of high degree, and strove with them as with
savage wild beasts, for the men tried to restrain her from making
the women do even as she had done: (forsaking) their worldly
rank and position. And she spoke to them thus:

> My children, four hundred years ago it was written that
> that time was the last time. Why do you hold fast thus
> strenuously to the vain love of the world? Take heed
> lest the day of Antichrist overtake you, and keep not fast
> hold upon your own riches and the possessions of your
> fathers.

And having set free all these she brought them to the life of the
ascetic and recluse.

In Palestine she rebuked an ascetic for washing his hands
and feet, and declared she had not washed any part of her body,
even her face, since becoming an ascetic. Nor has she slept in
a bed. However, she is fond of reading and reads Gregory
(Nazianzen?), Pierius, Basil, "and of other writers, more than
two hundred and fifty thousand sayings. And she did not read
them in an ordinary fashion just as she came to them, and she
did not hurry over them in an easy and pleasant manner, but
with great labor and understanding she used to read each book
seven or eight times. And because of this she was enabled, by
being set free from lying doctrine, to fly by means of the gift of
learning to great opinions, and she made herself a spiritual bird,

and in this wise was taken up to Christ her Lord."[2] Note in all this a spirit of aversion and estrangement from the world.

St. Melania the Younger

Melania the Younger, granddaughter of the above, was born in Rome in 383. Married at fourteen, she adopted a penitent life after the death of two sons, eventually accomplishing the total liquidation of an immense fortune. She met with opposition from Roman society. In 406, she moves to Nola with St. Paulinus. Her husband goes with her. In 408, she goes to Sicily with Rufinus, and in 410, to her properties in Africa where she begins a friendship with Augustine. In 413, she travels to Jerusalem via Egypt and settles on the Mount of Olives, where she imitates Egyptian hermits. She founds a convent of virgins on the Mount of Olives, near the Basilica of the Ascension, and lives an intense life of prayer and penance. She died in 440.

Roman Monasticism in Palestine

1) It is dominated by the influence of Nitria and Scete, i.e., by hermits. [See above; see below.]

2) There is an attraction to the Holy Places—monks and nuns furnish choirs for churches at the Holy Places in Bethlehem, Jerusalem (N.B. *Roman* Liturgy).

3) There is a preponderance of *nuns*.

4) There is a strong influence of Jerome (positive or negative)—hence the importance of study and intellectual activity.

---

[2] *The Paradise or Garden of the Holy Fathers: Being Histories of the Anchorites, Recluses, Monks, Coenobites, and Ascetic Fathers of the Deserts of Egypt between A.D. CCL and A.D. CCCC Circiter*, ed. and trans. Ernest A. Wallis Budge, 2 vols. (London: Chatto & Windus, 1907), 1:160 (slightly revised).

5) These communities exercised an influence by letters on the West, and attracted visitors from there. Jerome received financial support from St. Exuperius, bishop of Toulouse.

We can now consider a few characteristic texts.

From the *Life of St. Melania the Younger* by Gerontius—her ascetic life in North Africa:

a) *Fasting* was extremely strict, a little liquid nourishment in the evening; at other times, she ate only on Saturdays and Sundays (dry bread and water)—"*Hebdomadary*" [adjective meaning, "for seven days"]. But when she began fasting in the Easter season her mother reproached her for ignoring the holy tradition (note well: the Eustathians were condemned for this at Gangres). "It is not right for a Christian to fast on the day of our Lord's Resurrection but one must take bodily nourishment along with the spiritual." Easter was extended through Paschal Time and to all Sundays of the year.

b) *Watching*: After sleeping two hours, she would wake the virgins living with her (mostly her former slaves), saying, "Just as the Blessed Abel and all the saints offered to God their first fruits, so let us also employ the first fruits of the night in glorifying God. For we must watch and pray at every hour, because we do not know when the thief will come." She gave the virgins strict rules of silence and directed them, having them manifest their thoughts to her.

c) *Lectio*: She read the whole Bible two or three times a year, copying out what was especially useful for her. She chose Thagaste in order to study Scripture there under Alypius, the friend of Augustine. She was "*philologos*"—a lover of literature, reading, and the Bible "was never out of her holy hands." She liked private recitation of the whole Psalter— she completed privately the psalms not said in Office that day (Daily Psalter). She was perfect in both Greek and Latin; she read all the Patristic treatises she could get.

d) *Austerity*: When she was rich, the embroidery of a rich garment she wore had scratched her tender skin and caused inflammation. But now she wore the *maphorion* [garment covering the head and shoulders] and cowl of coarse hair cloth. She had obtained strength from the Lord by prayer. "Ask and you shall receive."

e) *Reclusion*: She wanted perpetual reclusion in North Africa but renounced it in order to maintain contact with people who needed her. But she spent a great part of her time in her cell, in solitude, lying in a box.

Her Monastic Life in the East

She went to the Holy Land as an integral part of *Sequela Christi* "the following of Christ." She meets St. Cyril at Alexandria. Reaching Jerusalem, she gives money in secret through others, and is registered among poor pilgrims. She lives at the Holy Sepulchre, praying there at night.

In Egypt, she tries to give gold to hermits, but is blocked by their refusals. She meets the Abbot of Tabenna, Victor, and visits Nitria and the desert of Cells. "The hermits received her as a man." On the Mount of Olives she retires to her mother's cell, and encloses herself there in sackcloth and ashes, after Epiphany. Then she builds a convent for about ninety nuns, with a special emphasis on rehabilitating fallen women.

[Her] ascetic teaching: Its basis is:

a) They have come to give their virginity to Christ, body and soul: *body*—total separation from the world of men; *soul*—vigilance in prayer, in fear and in the presence of angels, avoiding all evil thoughts (note the Evagrian background).

b) All ascesis is based on *purity of love* for God and one another. Without this their asceticism is false. The devil can imitate all the virtues but not love and humility.

c) Faith is the essential foundation of all true ascesis.

[Her] practice entails the following:

a) She has them fast, but would guard against pride in fasting. Hence fasting is "the last of the virtues" and for its merit depends on obedience. To neglect other virtues and depend on fasting alone is like a bride who appears in old clothes but only has a pair of very fine shoes. However, they must persevere in fasting with joy and be generous in it. They must enter by this narrow gate.

b) Obedience "consists in this: doing what you do not like to do, for the satisfaction of the one who commands you, and doing violence to yourself for the sake of Christ."

c) Liturgy. They rose at night after a short sleep, "Not having satisfied one's desire for sleep"—but then returned to bed afterwards. Night Office consisted in "Three responsories, three lessons and fifteen antiphons"; there were also "Morning Office" (Lauds); Tierce "because then the Paraclete came upon the Apostles"; Sext "because then Abraham received the Lord"; None "when Peter and John went to the Temple"; Vespers, a time of "special fervor— the hour when the disciples of Emmaus travelled with Christ, the Hour of *peace*." There was Mass on Friday, Sunday and Feasts. The church contained relics of Zachary, St. Stephen, and the forty martyrs of Sebaste.

Monasticism in Mesopotamia and Syria

ere the ascetic element is even more emphasized. The monks of Palestine and Mesopotamia in general were more rigid and extreme than the monks of Egypt. Theodoret of Cyrrhus is the main source for information about these monks. [For instance:]

1) St. James of Nisibis, bishop, d. 361, hermit and then bishop—typical of Syrian monasticism—lived on wild herbs, without fixed abode, slept in a cave in winter, outdoors in summer.

2) St. Aphraates, a Persian abbot and then bishop.

3) St. Ephrem, deacon, lived temporarily as anchorite outside Edessa, [a] famous Syrian liturgical poet.

4) St. John Chrysostom lived for a time (six years) as monk and hermit alternately, outside Antioch and wrote in defense of monastic life and on compunction. He is noted more as bishop and Doctor, defender of orthodoxy. We shall see later that he welcomes Cassian and Egyptian Origenist monks to Constantinople.

The Stylites

The Stylites—column sitters—first made their appearance in Syria. St. Symeon Stylites, born in Antioch, died 459, is one of the great saints of the fifth century. He first chained himself to a rock, then got a pillar ten feet high, changed to one thirty feet high and finally on one sixty-three feet high, renowned throughout the world for his miracles. After the death of Symeon there was a bitter struggle for his relics between the Patriarch of Antioch and the monks who had settled around his pillar. [The] Patriarch got them with the help of soldiers. But afterwards the relics were taken to Constantinople. A huge basilica was built around the abandoned pillar and was a great center of pilgrimages, comparable to Lourdes or Fatima today. Celebrations were held there in 1959—fifteenth centenary of his death.

How did stylites live? St. Symeon spent thirty-seven years on top of pillars—thirty of them on the sixty-three-foot pillar. He stood without shelter, protected by a railing. He prayed with *metaniae* (repeated genuflections). A pilgrim once counted up to 1,244 successive prostrations. He was tied to a post in Lent when he fasted the whole forty days. Other stylites had shelters. Food was hauled up in a basket, provided by faithful and disciples. They preached to the crowds, gave spiritual direction. Those who wanted a "private" interview went up a ladder. Pilgrims came from all over the world: Gaul, Britain, Turkestan.

Other stylites: St. Daniel, St. Symeon the Younger, St. Jonas. Attempts at stylitism in the West were stopped by bishops.

What attitude should we take toward this kind of sanctity? The fashion has been to disparage it, to treat it as something absurd and grotesque. This is not the full truth. It was a witness to the divine transcendency, and to the superiority of the spirit. Precisely its uselessness was what made this witness powerful. If we are to fully understand our contemplative vocation, we must be able to understand the uselessness, the "folly" of the stylites. The folly of God is greater than the wisdom of men. It was a protest against the worldly preoccupation with politics, and politico-theological struggles, with earthly and ecclesiastical ambition, etc. Symeon converted thousands of pagans.

However, it must be admitted that the monasticism of Palestine and Syria represents an extreme against which St. Benedict himself is clearly in reaction. We have a story of St. Benedict reproving a hermit who chained himself to a rock. St. Benedict inveighed against the independence and irresponsibility of monks who wandered about without superiors. The Sarabaites and Gyrovagues flourished mostly in Syria—monks without ecclesiastical control. Great deviations occurred, and monasticism would quickly have been ruined if there had not been intervention on the part of men like St. Basil to bring in sobriety and organization. On the other hand, we must not imagine that Basilian monasticism was something tightly and rigidly organized either. But there was the control of obedience and the sobering influence of discretion.

Hermits of Nitria and Scete

We now come to the heart of our subject: the great monastic centers of northern Egypt, where Cassian and Germanus wandered about consulting the "old men"—the land of the *Apothegmata* ["Sayings"], and of the other famous Desert Father texts. First, let us list summarily the more famous collections of stories, proverbs, and other Desert Father material. This is in addition to the Life of Anthony, etc. mentioned above.

1) *Historia Monachorum*, translated by Rufinus.

2) *Historia Lausiaca*, by Palladius, disciple of St. John Chrysostom—gets its name from the fact that it was dedicated to Lausus, chamberlain of Theodosius II. Dom C. Butler made a famous English translation and edition (1904). It was written before Cassian's *Conferences*, in 419–20.

3) *The Apothegmata* ["Sayings"] or *Verba Seniorum*. This is without doubt the best source for the spirituality of the Desert Fathers, better even than Cassian. Its advantages:

a) This collection represents predominantly the spirit of the hermits of Scete, and Scete was the center of the purest and most perfect eremitism in Egypt.

b) It is completely simple and colloquial, without frills or decorations, and seems to go back faithfully to the actual manner of expression of the Fathers themselves. In doing so, it gives us a picture not of exalted and extraordinary men living in an atmosphere of marvelous spiritual events, but of simple and humble hermits fleeing everything savoring of pride and display, preferring all that is obscure and unobtrusive.

c) It is concerned with the spiritual life and not with strange and marvelous tales.

d) The Fathers are content to confine themselves exclusively to practical and simple matters of everyday life. They generally refuse even to venture a comment on Scripture or any form of theological doctrine. They just discuss the ways of confronting problems of ascetic life.

e) The stories are taken from life, many of them consisting simply of "words of salvation" or fragments of spiritual advice given by a master to a disciple.

f) The doctrine of the *Apothegmata* is marked above all by its simplicity and discretion. It is a doctrine that can be followed and is basically healthy, as opposed to the exaggerations that are found in some of the other sources.

g) The *Apothegmata* are more purely *Coptic*. The other sources represent mixtures from Syrian and other Oriental sources. We can distinguish clearly between the humble and practical spirituality of the original Coptic monks, and the intellectualism of Evagrius, for instance, Macarius also.

Apothegmata, properly so called, "words of salvation," [are] brief proverbial statements, and longer stories with a practical moral, illustrating a truth about the hermit life.

Characteristics of Desert Spirituality

The primary concern of the desert life is to seek God, to seek salvation. The salutation common among Desert Fathers was "*sotheis*"—mayest thou be saved. Many of the sentences are simply answers to the question, "What ought I to do?" Hence the answers are simple, succinct summaries of some of the main obligations of a monk in the primitive sense.

But remember, these were bits of advice given to individuals; hence they are responses to special individual needs, and are not in themselves the universal answer to all questions. They must be pieced together and seen in perspective—must be seen in light of special circumstances.

[And] remember that there was no set rule for the hermit—only certain rather free prevalent customs. He had to make his own rule of life, based on the individual teaching and advice received from the Fathers. He had to know what to accept and what to discard as useless to him. The memorable phrases which have been preserved are remarkable not so much for their special depth, as for the fact that someone was struck very deeply by them and held on to them as coming from God. They became a rule of life for *him*.

There was no irresponsible license in the true Desert Fathers. The Desert Fathers were not necessarily magic directors, wizard gurus, who had a series of infallible answers on all points. They were humble and sagacious men, of few words, whom the Holy Ghost used for His purposes. We must know how to take advantage of direction in this sense. If we seek our director as a kind of oracle, he will always fail us. If we are prepared to listen to him in simplicity and accept, with faith, some ordinary observation of his as coming from God, then he will be able to help us. This faith requires not absolute blindness of the reason and common sense: it requires a certain trust and response on our part, an awareness that this is fitting for our case, which faith intensifies and enables us to see in an entirely supernatural light. For this, we must be open and trusting. We must be able to let go a little. If we cannot trust any director, then we will have more trials and difficulties. Confidence in a director is a grace to be prayed for. In any case we all should be attentive to special "words of salvation" that come to us in reading, sermons, conferences or direction, as God's special words for us.

What should the monk do? [Here are] a few examples taken at random from our small collection *What Ought I to Do?*[1] A general summary of the virtues of monastic life: .

> An elder said: Here is the monk's life-work / obedience / meditation / not judging others / not reviling / not complaining. For it is written: You who love the Lord / hate evil. So this is the monk's life—not to walk in agreement with an unjust man / nor to look with his eyes upon evil / not to go about being curious / and neither to examine nor to listen to the business of others. Not to take anything with his hands / but rather to give to others. Not to be proud in his heart / nor to malign others in his thoughts. Not to fill his stomach / but in all things to behave with discretion. Behold / in all this you have the monk.

Have no confidence in your own virtuousness, do not worry about a thing once it has been done, control your tongue and your belly.

---

[1] *What Ought I to Do? Sayings of the Desert Fathers*, trans. Thomas Merton (Lexington, KY: Stamperia del Santuccio, 1959). "This limited edition of 100 sayings from the *Verba Seniorum* was later published in an expanded edition of 150 sayings as *The Wisdom of the Desert: Sayings from the Desert Fathers of the Fourth Century* (New York: New Directions, 1960)." –Patrick O'Connell

This saying of St. Anthony is simple and wise, basic—humility, trust, and temperance. Note the wisdom of the Desert Fathers who insist on not worrying about things that can no longer be changed. What is done is done. Don't fret over it, but do not do it again—true penance.

* To accept illness and temptation with thanksgiving.

* Purity of intention and obedience.

* Work—the monk must not be idle—but must spend his life in solitary work supporting himself and aiding the weaker brethren.

* Silence—meaning not mutism but wise control of speech, especially refraining from all vainglory in talk, all showing off knowledge, all desire to prove one's point or justify oneself. Silence is for the sake of contemplation—cf. Arsenius, *"Fuge, tace, quiesce."* "Fly, be silent, and rest in prayer." Arsenius reminds us that the monk is above all one who renounces the world and flies from it. Why? Because possessions lay one open to attacks of demons. Hence importance of poverty, and even strict poverty in the monastic life itself—no compromise with spirit of proprietorship, even in the best and most necessary of things. One should not have anything he is not willing to part with, even if it is taken violently and unjustly.

* Hence *solitude*: one must "stay in the cell, the cell will teach you all things." The desert life should lead to contemplation, but by the way of humility. A monk should not just be content with his little ascetic routine: he should seek to become "all fire." He should be "all eye like the cherubim and seraphim."

But the way to contemplation is barred by insuperable obstacles, in anyone who is uncharitable and despises others, who is attached to exterior penance for its own sake, or is in any way proud, attached to himself, noisy, turbulent, arrogant, etc. The hallmark of the true saint in the desert as everywhere else is *charity*. And this simple charity is both active and passive: active in the sense that it is all ready to perform works of mercy, when the occasion arises, and passive in the sense that it supports every injury and trial with heroic patience. The charity of the Desert Fathers is outstanding and it is what most impresses the readers of the *Verba Seniorum*. In other collections, their asceticism and miracles tend to be more prominent.

Some other characteristics of desert spirituality:

The quality of being a stranger or an exile, a man without any fixed abode or home, in the likeness of Christ who had nowhere to rest His head. But this includes stability in a cell, except certain cases like Bessarion who "wandered about the desert without any more cares than a bird of the heavens [but always stayed in the same general area, otherwise no stability] . . . no house, no desire to travel, no books . . . entirely freed from all bodily desires, resting only on the firmness of his faith."

Anachoresis—solitude. The Desert Fathers repeat the Neoplatonic maxim, "alone with the Alone," *solus ad Solum*. This does not exclude charity as we have seen. Solitude, with work and prayer, forms one of the three great obligations of the desert monk. These three together are his very life itself. But solitude is combined with the strict obligation of hospitality and instruction. The guest sent by God is to be received as Christ Himself, and entertained. The obligation of fasting yields to the primary obligation of charity; one breaks fast to eat with [a] guest. A disciple or a tempted brother must be counseled and helped.

Humility—is the essence of charitable social relations, on both sides.

Penthos—Compunction, also is of the very essence of desert spirituality, allied with fear of the Lord and humility: against useless and empty laughter. The life of the Desert Father is serious, and *penthos* is an instrument for interiority. It drives one into the depths, makes one thoughtful, hesitant to trust in his own words and opinions, ready to listen, aware of his failings. But it is combined with courage and hope in God. It is not mere morbid pessimism. Abbot Isaias was told by Abbot Macarius: "Flee from men" (this was a word of salvation) but he asked for explanation. Fleeing from men, according to Macarius, implies "to remain seated in your cell and to bewail your sins." Hence the connection between *penthos* and *anachoresis, euche* (prayer) and humility—also stability. This shows the important and vital interconnection between all the virtues in an organic whole, in the desert life. Note also, devotion to Our Lord and to the Blessed Mother is connected with *penthos*. Abbot Poemen comes out of ecstasy and says: "My spirit was there where holy Mary the Mother of God, wept at the foot of the Savior's Cross. And I would very much like always to weep like that." This sort of thing, thought to be characteristic of *devotio moderna*, is often found in the simplicity of the Desert Fathers.

Diakrisis—Discretion. As we have seen from St. Anthony, discretion is the most important virtue in the monastic life because without it all the others go astray. This is also the teaching of St. Thomas [Aquinas] on Prudence.

Amerimnia—The absence of all cares, especially material ones. This was sometimes an impossible ideal (cf. John the Dwarf).

Hesychia—As we have seen above, "*quies*" or sweet repose in contemplation is the crown of the desert life, the reward of all the hermit's strivings and the foretaste of heaven. But the Fathers were very simple and retiring about this also; they did not seek to be known or admired for their prayer but to keep it hidden and consequently they have little to say about it. However, there were great speculative theologians in the desert, notably Macarius and especially Evagrius. It is time to consider these theologians of contemplation.

St. Macarius and Pseudo-Macarius

St. Macarius

There were two saints by this name in the desert, contemporaries and friends. The first was a monk of Nitria, Macarius of Alexandria, called "*politikos*," the "city man." He left no writings. (A third, Macarius of Magnesia, is sometimes confused with these two.) Macarius the Great, the one who concerns us, was practically the founder of Scete and was the master of Evagrius of Pontus. Hence he is really the fountainhead of the desert school of mystical theology.

He was born about 300–310. He lived to be ninety years old. He came to Scete when he was 30 and became famous for miracles and prophecies—was ordained priest on this account at the age of 41. In Migne there are many works ascribed to Macarius, but most of them are almost certainly by someone else. For example, there are some fifty homilies, which seem to have been written for cenobites, and are said to have Messalian tendencies, belong to a later date, some monk of Asia Minor or Syria. There are also treatises (which are just selections from the homilies) and letters. The *Epistola ad Monachos* was long thought to be genuine, but even this is almost certainly not by Macarius. In Greek manuscripts the author is called Macarius, but now the same letter in Arabic is ascribed to one Symeon. Who was he? A shorter version of the same letter was also ascribed to St. Ephrem. The *Epistola ad Monachos*, ascribed to Macarius, deals with the ideal of the monastic life, the "conversion" to that true good which man desires by his very nature and which God makes accessible to him by grace. He considers *the way of perfection* in the spiritual life, especially *apatheia* and the need for humility. Prayer he says is the leader of all the choir of virtues.

[This] is the proper spirituality of monks and contemplatives, although rather limited in its views. It is an early psychology of the contemplative life. But we must realize that there are other very important perspectives which are omitted.

Messalianism

In addition to the letters ascribed to Macarius the Great, which are few in number, there remain a large number of homilies ascribed to him. For a long time it was thought that the letters were really by Macarius and the homilies by some unknown Messalian. Werner Jaeger has shown that both are by the same person, an admirer and copier of Gregory of Nyssa, probably some Syrian cenobite of the fifth century. Now these Macarian homilies are important for the history of Oriental spirituality because of the great influence they had on the development of the Hesychast movement. Hence it is necessary here to consider the teachings on prayer of the homilies of Pseudo-Macarius. But since these homilies are full of Messalian tendencies, we have to stop first of all to consider the meaning of the Messalian heresy.

Messalianism [is] a heresy which gave exaggerated emphasis to prayer and to the sensible experiences that occur during prayer. For the Messalians, contemplation and the quasi-physical experience of "divine things" was all-important, and the sign of true spiritual perfection. Without such "experiences" no real perfection was possible. Such subjective experiences outweighed in importance the liturgical and sacramental life of the Church. By experiences of prayer one was sanctified and made perfect. It was condemned in a general way at the Council of Ephesus

(431). The heretical doctrines of the Messalians were summarized and condemned by St. John Damascene, Theodoret, and others. Briefly, the main errors of the Messalians were these:

1) Original sin gave the devil possession of man's inmost heart, so that everyone is born possessed by the devil. Baptism itself is powerless to deliver man from this state of possession. But perpetual prayer is able to get the devil out of man's heart and leads eventually to complete possession by the Holy Spirit. Hence it is a perpetual spiritual prayer which is the main sanctifying force in man's life.

2) In order to practice perpetual prayer, they neglect work and remain in a state of silence and inertia for long periods (i.e., overemphasis on a quietistic type of contemplation); in this contemplation they claim to see God with the eyes of the body at certain times—at other times they are moved to sudden impulsive actions, dancing, "shaking," etc. and "shooting imaginary arrows" at the devils.

3) By the practice of perpetual prayer one arrived at *apatheia*, complete immunity to all passion. One also arrived at mystical marriage with the Divine Spouse, which was in some way physically experienced. Not only that but the soul and body are completely transformed into God so as to become really divine, having a divine nature. They claimed full sensible awareness of the indwelling Spirit, also of sin and of grace.

4) There were also several dogmatic errors, concerning the Trinity, Incarnation, etc. They allowed women to be "priests" among them, if they were "spiritual" or enlightened. They neglected the Eucharist, and also taught, as some quietists, that the "perfect" could sin bodily without being affected spiritually.

Traces and tendencies of this kind of teaching are found in the Pseudo-Macarian homilies, and also recur in later Oriental mystical writings. For instance Symeon the New Theologian places great emphasis on the sensible experience of divine light. However, the errors thus presented in a crude form must not mislead us when we read the Orthodox mystics: words must be carefully weighed, and the Hesychasts (those who experienced sweetness and rest) are not all to be treated automatically as Messalians. But the fact remains that the hesychast aspiration to *experience* in full the divine light can be misleading, especially when this experience is described as quasi-physical.

Pseudo-Macarius

It is still hotly disputed whether the writer of the homilies by "Macarius" was really a Messalian or not. However, it has been shown that the Homilies of Pseudo-Macarius, while sounding Messalian, are really not so. (Problem of establishing what is really Messalian—no original Messalian documents exist, and one has to judge by what those who condemned it alleged that it was.)

Recently, the spirituality and the heritage of Pseudo-Macarius have been defended by [John] Meyendorff (authority on Gregory Palamas) who contrasts two trends in Oriental Christian mysticism:

1) Platonist, intellectualist and pagan, stemming from Evagrius Ponticus.

2) Biblical, stemming from Pseudo-Macarius. This distinction is based on two different views of man. In the former it is the mind, *nous*, that is the seat of spirituality and of prayer. In the latter it is the "heart" which stands for the whole man, body and soul spiritualised by grace.

This follows the Biblical terminology in which the "heart" is regarded as the psycho-physiological center of man, and the seat of his deepest, most spiritual powers. The first kind of spirituality regards man as a mind imprisoned in matter. The second takes man as a whole, and is entirely sanctified by grace.

Two ways of prayer follow from this. The Evagrian line leads to highly intellectual contemplation, in which the body has no part. The Macarian line leads to the "Prayer of the Heart," familiar at Mount Athos, the "Prayer of Jesus" in which the body has a place in prayer. This is sometimes compared to yoga, and condemned, as "Christian Yoga."[1] But it must be studied carefully before it can be condemned. We have not yet reached the point where we can give final judgement in this matter. It is of great contemporary interest in spiritual theology.

[1] "Meyendorff stresses that despite a similarity in technique, the Christian 'prayer of the breath' places strong emphasis on the necessity of grace and on a sacramental context." –Patrick O'Connell

Evagrius Ponticus on Prayer

One of the great masters at Scete in the time of Cassian was Evagrius of Pontus. He was generally considered as the greatest theologian of the desert, and was a follower of Origen.

He is indeed one of the fathers of Christian mystical theology. He came from Asia Minor (Pontus) and was a friend of St. Basil and a disciple of St. Gregory Nazianzen. He lived in the "desert of cells." He died on the feast of the Epiphany, 399. After his death the great Origenist conflict broke out, leading to the departure of the Origenists from Scete. The memory of Evagrius was blackened and he then fell into oblivion.

In the earlier works on Desert Monasticism, Evagrius has a good name and is regarded as a holy and learned father. In the later works, after the fifth century, he has a very bad reputation. Moschus, [in his] *Spiritual Meadow*, records a story that his cell was said to be haunted or inhabited by a devil. He also said that he was in hell among the heretics. St. John Climacus condemns him. In general this is due to the fact that he was a noted Origenist and he fell with the Origenist party, thereafter stigmatised as a "deviationist." Yet his work not only survived, but strongly influenced even those who despised his memory. St. Maximus the Confessor, one of the great mystics among the Fathers, while twice condemning Evagrius by name, nevertheless is not only full of Evagrian doctrines, but can even be said to base his whole doctrine on Evagrius.

There are some works of Evagrius in Migne's *Patrologia Graeca*: the *Practicos*, the *Mirror of Monks*, the *Letter to Anatolios*. But more works of his are preserved in Syrian and Armenian and are more recently studied. Another mystic influenced by him is Isaac of Nineveh, a Nestorian bishop and theologian who is also beginning to interest students in the West. Isaac calls Evagrius "the Blessed Mar Evagrios," "the wise one among the saints," "prince of gnostics." Note: Isaac of Nineveh, full of Evagrius, was translated into Greek and much influenced Byzantine tradition; the translators, where Isaac praised Evagrius, simply inserted some other name, like Gregory of Nazianz.

Importance of Evagrius

His systematic presentation of the great theology of the first Fathers, especially Origen and Gregory of Nyssa, [was] in a form that became definitive in the East. He is really the cornerstone of Oriental mystical theology, a cornerstone that was rejected. We have seen that St. Maximus is based on Evagrius. So is the Pseudo-Denys (6th cent.). Even John Climacus is largely based on Evagrius.

The chief work of Evagrius, the *De Oratione*, ["On Prayer"] survived and was very popular—but it was ascribed to St. Nilus. It exercised very considerable influence. The teaching of Cassian on prayer is very similar to that of Evagrius; indeed it is a kind of digest of the more profound and complete treatise of the Master. It will greatly aid us to understand the monastic tradition on prayer if we acquaint ourselves a little with Evagrius. The treatise is perfectly free from suspect "Origenism" and is one of the great Christian texts on interior prayer.

On Prayer consists of a Prologue and 153 short *capitula*. Earlier than the works of Pseudo-Denys, this treatise of Evagrius definitively set the course for the mysticism of the Oriental Church. "It is through Evagrius that the great ideas of Origen and Gregory of Nyssa came down from their inaccessible heights to the level of the average intelligence," says Father Hausherr.

What Does Evagrius Mean by Prayer?

He is talking of what we would call mental prayer. He distinguishes prayer and psalmody. These are necessarily distinct and complementary, according to Evagrius. They are the two wings of the eagle, by which we ascend into the heights (*Oratione* 82— all the numbers given in brackets, unless otherwise stated, refer to *capitula* of the *De Oratione*). Psalmody belongs more to the active life; it "appeases the passions and lulls the intemperance of the body" (83). It is a more active and exterior form of devotion, and quantity is more important than in "*oratio*," which is interior, contemplative, and depends more on quality. In particular, the function of psalmody is to calm the passions, and especially anger. Prayer (*oratio*) is the exercise of the intelligence in a purely interior and spiritual contact with God (*Oratione* 3). Psalmody belongs more properly to the lower degrees of the spiritual life, prayer to the higher (85). Evagrius speaks of both prayer and psalmody less as practices than as charisms, which are to be prayed for as special gifts from God (87).

We must not however think of prayer as purely spiritual and always without words or concepts or acts. On the contrary, in time of temptation especially, prayer is to be "short and intense"—acts (with or without words) having the character of ejaculations (98). Although prayer is higher than psalmody, Evagrius does not mean that one leaves psalmody behind altogether and ascends to a life of "pure prayer" that is continuous and without any exterior practices. However, when on occasion one has arrived at a deep interior contact with God, one should not abandon it merely because one has previously determined to recite psalms. One should not let go of what is better in order to revert to a mechanical practice. So he says: "If a profitable thought comes to thee, let it take the place of psalmody. Do not reject the gift of God merely in order to cling to the traditions of men," etc.

Prayer defined: Mental and contemplative prayer is for Evagrius primarily an activity of the intellect, and is the highest activity of this faculty. In this intellectualist emphasis Evagrius is later corrected by St. Maximus who gives more place to charity in contemplation; but note that Evagrius's contemplation is not exclusively intellectual. However the chief characteristic of Evagrius is that for him the monk is one who seeks above all a *continuous state of intellectual contemplation*. Everything else in Evagrius is ordered to this supreme end. Intellectual contemplation is the fruit and the expression of perfect charity and it is what love seeks exclusively and above all. It is pure prayer that makes man "equal to the angels" and one must leave all else, he says, in order to seek this blessed angelic state. Angels are *pure intelligence* and the contemplative also tends to be "all eyes" (in contemplation) or "all fire." Such also is the true "theologian." In contemplation man also returns to his first, pure, paradisiacal state.

Oratione 3—"Prayer is a conversation of the intellect with God . . . without intermediary." The word "conversation" must not lead us into error here: he is not thinking of words, nor even of thoughts, for the highest prayer is an intellectual contact with God, in a direct intuition (not however clear vision), that is beyond words and thoughts. This definition however covers various degrees of prayer, including a lower degree of supplication which takes the form of ejaculatory acts in time of struggle, as we have already seen above. The lower kind of pure prayer is merely disinterested petition. The higher kind is prayer without concept or image. Pure prayer, prayer without intermediary, means not a pure intuition in the sense of the beatific vision, but an intuition of God that does not require the mediation of a created object, angel, or even the sacred humanity of Jesus. The degrees of purity in prayer are degrees of immediacy. The highest prayer is intellectual intuition of the Holy Trinity. Other degrees, as we shall see, involve the intuition of spiritual beings, such as angels.

The first degrees of prayer demand purification from passionate thought. The highest degree demands perfect "nudity" of the intellect clothed in no thought at all. The lower degrees of "pure prayer" are compatible with suffering and sorrow. In the higher degrees there is only peace, tranquillity, and joy. But no pure prayer is compatible with inordinate passion or with any vice. In another place he says the highest perfection of the intellect is prayer without distraction (34a): "Prayer without distraction is the highest operation of the intelligence."

The object of the life of prayer is to ascend from the valley of shadows, attachment to passionate thoughts, to the summit of the mountain of contemplation of the Holy Trinity. In the lower degrees of prayer we are more engaged in "supplicating" to be purified. After first renouncing things themselves we begin by begging to be purified of passions. Then, in the intermediate stage, we ask to be purified of ignorance. Finally, in order to reach the summit, we need to be purified of all darkness and dereliction. In other words, the spiritual life is an ascent to greater and greater spiritual purity and intellectual clarity (37).

However, Evagrius and his followers agree that those who reach the heights of contemplation are very rare and even fervent monks spend their whole lives trying (vainly) to completely conquer "passionate thoughts"—few ever get to the degree where they struggle directly with ignorance or darkness. When he reaches the summit the contemplative has reached the highest dignity for which the intelligence was created—for God made the mind of man in order that we might contemplate the Most Holy Trinity. This highest act of the intelligence, contemplation of the Holy Trinity, leads to pure love (118).

Degrees of Prayer Summary

1) *Preliminaries*: In order to enter upon the life of prayer one must be detached from objects. Evagrius distinguishes

detachment from objects and from the thoughts of objects. Here we are pretty much on the same ground as in Cassian, *Conference 3*.

2) *Apatheia*—The true life of prayer begins when one has not only left behind the things of earth, but is beginning the struggle with thoughts of those things. The first step in the life of prayer is the struggle with "passionate thoughts," i.e., thoughts that move us to passion, whether anger, lust, etc. Here, meditation is important, including the constant meditation of death and the last things, until the soul begins to be free. Here the big thing is virtue. Note—combat with evil spirits is crucial. According to Evagrius (*Or.* 49), the chief purpose of the battle waged by devils against the monk is to prevent or to frustrate interior prayer. The devils tempt us to those vices most contrary to prayer, especially lust and anger. *Apatheia* is the victory of the soul over all the devils (i.e., all the passions). Note that *apatheia* is not mere insensibility. It is compounded of humility, compunction, zeal, and intense love for God. *Apatheia* is the state of a soul that is no longer moved by passionate thought. The thoughts of such souls are "simple," that is to say, untainted by passion: they have no "charge" of passion in them; we simply see objects as they are, in simplicity. At this point one reaches the stage of "meditation on simple thoughts." Note that prayer is inseparably connected with virtue. Without virtue, one cannot resist passion, and if one is dominated by passion, he has no control of thoughts and cannot pray. However, Evagrius always insists that prayer is *a pure gift of God*; it is not attained by our own ascetic efforts but we must beg Him for the gift of prayer (*Or.* 58).

3) *Spiritual Contemplation—Gnosis* and *Theoria Physica*. The mind is now beyond simple thoughts but it receives in itself the form of the essences of things—an intuitive penetration of reality—of "nature" in so far as it reflects

God. This, in other words, is an intuition of the Creator in His Creation. The *logoi* of creatures are reflections of the divine attributes. He says that in *theoria physica* we "receive letters" from God, but in the highest contemplation we speak to Him and He speaks to us. (Cf. St. John of the Cross, *Spiritual Canticle*, 2:3.) In the highest contemplation God is present directly to the mind without form or concept. In "Spiritual Contemplation" (*gnosis*), though the soul possesses *apatheia*, the devil can still tempt it—but now not with passions—rather he injects into the mind spiritual forms, images and visions which claim to "represent" God or divine things (*Or.* 67–68). In the highest contemplation (*Theologia*) the soul is beyond the reach of the devil because it no longer uses any concepts whatever and is pure of "all forms," and cannot be deceived by any false idea. This supposes that it is directly illuminated by God. How? It is not clearly explained.

4) *Theologia*—Union with God without intermediary of His creatures. The mind is now above all essences. (Cf. Ruysbroeck, *Spiritual Espousals*). *Or.* 60: "If you are a theologian you will truly pray and if you pray truly you are a theologian." For Evagrius: Theologian equals Mystic.

[So], is Evagrius dangerous? Evagrius is an extremist and several dangers are often pointed out in his teaching:

Angelism: There is a possibility that his doctrine on purity of prayer may tempt people to the idea that man is capable of living like a pure spirit without a body and without passions, and that the perfection to which we should tend is superhuman—total spiritualism. Does he ignore the reality of man? And despise God's Creation?

Is his doctrine pagan (Platonist) rather than Christian? Certainly there are many Platonic elements in it and Christ appears very little in it, almost not at all. However, the Holy Spirit plays a central role.

There is danger of pride and self-sufficiency. It is not altogether true that Evagrius exaggerates man's ascetic power and underestimates grace. But it is a spirituality centered on one's own purity and perfection. In the long run Evagrius is too idealistic and presents a program that is inaccessible to men.

There is truth in all these criticisms, but they are not absolute. They must be taken with a grain of salt, too. Evagrius can usually be interpreted in a way that gives his doctrine value for all time, and for the whole Church. It is a high contemplative ideal, aspiring perhaps to an exaggerated spiritual perfection which is not preached in the Gospel. In any case, the Evagrian ideal is what Cassian encountered in the desert, tempered by the simplicity of the more humble Desert Fathers as we have seen it in the *Apothegmata*.

Master of the Spiritual Life: Cassian

He is *the* great monastic writer—the Master of the spiritual life par excellence for monks—the source for all in the West. He is a classic, profoundly attached to tradition. He is a perfect source for the whole tradition of Oriental monasticism—basically the doctrine of Origen, adapted for monks by Evagrius—resuming all that we have so far discussed in Patristic thought.

He is remarkable for his grasp of the essentials of monasticism, avoiding bizarre details, in contrast to Palladius, for example. He is not a mere compiler—he shows real literary talent and ability to organize ideas in an original synthesis valid for all. He propagated in the West the doctrine of active and contemplative lives. He is interesting, human, a good observer and psychologist, a prudent Master of the spiritual life; every monk should know him thoroughly.

He influenced all the early monastic founders in the West, including St. Honoratus of Lérins, St. Caesarius; in Spain, St. Isidore, and St. Fructuosus. He even influenced the early monks of Ireland. In the East he is revered by all—called a saint. He is included in the *Philokolia* and praised by St. John Climacus as "The Great Cassian." In modern times, after influencing St. Thomas, Cassian also had a profound effect on St. Ignatius and the Jesuits, on De Rancé and the Trappists, on Port Royal, on Fenelon.

St. Benedict considers Cassian and [the] Desert Fathers ideal reading material for Compline. It is due to Cassian that the Compline reading exists and from his work it gets its name *Collatio*. Compline reading has a special formative importance in St. Benedict's eyes. It draws the monks together after the varying business of the day and brings them face to face with the essentials of their vocation, before they retire for the night. The Compline reading is designed especially for recollection and edification. Hence, St. Benedict considered Cassian an ideal author for monks, one who would help them lead their monastic lives more perfectly, one who would bring them into contact with God, for Whom they had left the world. In chapter 73, admitting that the *Rule* is a map for the "active life" of beginners, and looking forward to the progress of his monks in contemplation, St. Benedict again recommends Cassian. He designates three kinds of reading that will help the monk reach the perfection of his vocation:

1) The Scriptures, "every page of which is a most accurate norm to live by."

2) The works of the Catholic Fathers, which enable us to go directly to God: *recto cursu*.

3) "The *Conferences* of the Fathers and the *Institutes* (i.e., the two main books of Cassian) and their lives, together with the Rule of our Holy Father St. Basil."

These are described as "examples of good-living and obedient monks, and instruments of virtue."

This is one of the things most striking about Cassian: lifelike portraits of the Desert Fathers. They remain "models for imitation." But, in what sense are they to be imitated? Not in all their exterior actions—impossible to us—not at all suited to our situation; not in all their attitudes—they were extremists—they were often quite wrong. They are to be followed in their *faith*, their love of Christ, their zeal for the monastic state, and their spirit of prayer and sacrifice. In reading the Desert Fathers one must discriminate, adapt, as did St. Benedict himself, who consciously and deliberately wrote a *Rule* which some of the Desert Fathers would have condemned as soft:

> The priest Cassian, who wrote about the formation of faithful monks, should be diligently read and frequently heard; in the beginning of our vocation, he said, eight principal vices ought to be avoided. This writer so skillfully describes the evil movements of man's soul, that he helps one to see and avoid faults, whereas before he was in confusion and did not know what they were. However, Cassian was rightly blamed by St. Prosper for his errors about free will, and so we advise that he should be taken cautiously in this matter, in which he was mistaken. (*Cassiodorus*)

Cassian fell into semi-Pelagianism, but this error only appears in one or two places, and the fact that Cassian continued, in spite of it, to be the standard reading of all monks, is only an additional proof of his great authority in the ascetic field. The saints and Fathers of St. Benedict's day and of the Middle Ages would never have tolerated any of the works of a man suspected of heresy, if they had not been convinced that his writings were of the greatest value and importance, that in general their orthodoxy was beyond reproach. Compare what happened to Evagrius, who only survived under another name. The name of Cassian was always held in the highest respect.

St. Dominic seized upon the writings of Cassian as a most apt means of learning how to become a saint of God: "He took up the book which is called the Conferences of the Fathers, and read it carefully. He set his mind to understand the things which he read therein, to feel them in his heart, and to carry them out in his actions. From this book he learned purity of heart, the way of contemplation, and the perfection of all virtues" (*Life of St. Dominic*). This gives us an idea how we ought to read Cassian.

Cassian's Error

Before we go on to the study of Cassian's doctrine, we may briefly dispose of the error in his teaching.

It is misleading to use the term "semi-Pelagianism" of Cassian, as if to imply that he sympathized with Pelagius and adopted a modification of his heretical doctrine. Cassian is closer to St. Augustine than he is to Pelagius. Book 12 of the *Instituta*, on pride, is probably directed against the Pelagians. In his anti-Nestorian writings, Cassian explicitly condemns Pelagius' denial of the Redemption. Pelagius held that man was entirely capable of achieving his own salvation, even after original sin, and that Jesus had come only as an "inspiration" and a "model of virtue." Cassian appears to teach that grace is necessary to achieve the perfection of sanctity, and to imply that without grace one can *begin the work* of our sanctification, but not bring it to completion—in other words, that without grace we can do *something* to save our souls. Cassian can, however, be defended from this error by texts in which he says that Jesus declared that he could do nothing of Himself and that *a fortiori* we must say the same:

> [Jesus] says, in the person of his assumed humanity, that he is able to do nothing of himself; and do we, dust and ashes, think that in those things that pertain to our salvation we do not need the help of God!

In the dispute about semi-Pelagianism, the argument centers around the *initium fidei*, the first step towards believing. The heretics held that man could take this first step without grace. Cassian, however, explicitly says in the third Conference that even the *initium salutis* is a gift of God (Conf. 3:10). Also, he says "Paul declared that the beginning of our conversion and faith, and the endurance of sufferings, is given to us by the Lord." (Conf. 3:15—cf. Phil. 1:29). The grace of God, he declares, is necessary every day and at every moment.

However, the most disputed text of Cassian on this point is in the thirteenth Conference, the one reproved by St. Prosper, a disciple of St. Augustine. In 432, Prosper wrote a direct attack on Cassian. His motive is to defend St. Augustine against those who attacked his works on grace by appealing to Cassian. Even in attacking Cassian, Prosper calls him a "priest who excels among all others," and he does not attribute the doctrine on grace directly to Cassian, but to the Desert Father (Chaeremon) whom he is quoting. He praises Cassian for starting out the thirteenth Conference with the statement that God is the principle not only of our good acts but also of our good thoughts—that man has need of grace in all things. However, the language of the thirteenth Conference later becomes erroneous. Cassian says (quoting Chaeremon), "When Divine Providence sees in us a beginning of good will . . . then God begins to give us grace." He immediately says that God has sown this seed, but seems also to leave a possibility that the seed might also have been sown by our own efforts. It is a "beginning of good will" that comes either from God or from ourselves. But there is no either/or. It must all come from God. Cassian, in the thirteenth Conference, adopts without criticism Chaeremon's doctrine that the first beginnings of salvation sometimes come from God and sometimes from man. Cassian's error on this point was not merely a question of hazy terminology, but he actually deviated from the true doctrine (of St. Augustine), seeking a "middle path" between Augustine and Pelagius. As a dogmatic theologian, then, Cassian failed on this point.

Cassian's Life and Background

His place of birth is unknown—speculations about it name him as native of southern France, Romania, etc. Syria is improbable as [a] birthplace. He was born about 360 or 365. In his early youth he entered a monastery at Bethlehem, before St. Jerome went there. He had already received a complete classical formation. Why did he choose a monastery at Bethlehem? Out of veneration for the mystery of the Divine Infancy, and faith in the efficacy of that mystery as a source of grace for monks. In other words, he did not merely pick this place because it had been made famous by Our Lord, or because it recalled His memory: but above all because of the efficacy of the mystery of His childhood. He perhaps entered the monastery at the same time as his friend Germanus, who accompanies him on his voyage to Egypt.

Monasticism had been imported to Palestine from Egypt by St. Hilarion in the first part of the fourth century. (See above.) Cassian arrived a few years after the death of St. Hilarion, who was one of the first monastic confessors to receive a liturgical cult like that of the martyrs. The monasteries of Palestine were *lauras*, not quite cenobia, but more compact than the hermit colonies of St. Anthony. Cassian and Germanus probably lived together in the same hut. Palestinian monasticism emphasized exterior practices more than did that of the Egyptians. Cassian frequently remarks that the Palestinian monks made perfection consist in austerity, in long prayers, and special mortifications, while the Egyptians had a better idea of the essence of perfection—union with God, but at the same time were often more austere than the monks of Palestine. When Cassian visited Egypt for the first time, around 385, his discovery of the spirit of the monks of the desert came to him as a revelation, and thereafter he could not think of returning permanently to Palestine. It is for us to catch from him something of the undying inspiration of the Desert Fathers.

Around 385, Cassian and Germanus received permission to visit Egypt. Cassian is about twenty years old. The length of their stay was not determined, but they had to make a vow that they would return. The vow was made in the Cave of the Nativity. Their first stay in Egypt was to last about seven years. They returned for another seven years. They land at Thennesys, in the Delta, and are met by a local bishop, and go to visit three solitaries who live in the marshes nearby (Panephysis): they are Chaeremon, Nesteros, and Joseph. These are the ones who supply material for the second part of the *Conferences*—11 to 17, including the thirteenth which contains the error on nature and grace.

In the opening chapters of Conference 11, Cassian describes his arrival in the Delta, among "those old monks whose age is evident from their bowed frame and whose holiness shines forth in their expression, so that the mere sight of them is a lesson to the beholders." They find the anchorites living on lonely islands in the salt marshes. [Abbot] Chaeremon, a hundred years old, is no longer able to walk upright. He excuses himself, and tries to avoid giving them lessons in asceticism, because he is no longer able to observe the full austerity of his rule.

Chaeremon then gives them conferences on the three ways of combating the vices and reaching the perfection of charity, which restores to the soul the image and likeness of God (Conf. 11 on Perfection). The first five chapters are introductory. This is the first conference Cassian and Germanus hear in Egypt. We are introduced to Chaeremon, living in the marshes, a man of very great age, humility and wisdom. They tell him they have come to learn something in order to make progress. This is the starting point. Chaeremon begins with the assumption that perfection means the overcoming of vices. This is axiomatic for Cassian and the Desert Fathers. But besides the mere fact of "not sinning," what constitutes the deeper perfection of the spiritual life is the motive, the way in which we avoid evil and do good. The various motives for not sinning and doing good are:

1) fear of hell or of violating the law;

2) hope of reward and of the good that we will enjoy as a result of virtue;

3) love of good and virtue as such, for their own sakes.

It is this third that constitutes perfection: doing good without fear and without any interested motive, out of "perfect love" that is centered on the good alone, or even on love alone. It is love for love's sake (that is, for God's sake). Chaeremon associates faith with fear (servile attitude), hope with the "mercenary" attitude, and charity with perfection. (This is of course the heart of St. Bernard's mystical theology, the climax of his sermons on the Canticle of Canticles. Pure love which "casteth out fear" is the way to wisdom, in which we act and are moved only "*saporem boni*"—see Cistercian Breviary, III Nocturn, Feast of St. Bernard.) When this love is present, there is perfect resemblance to God Who gives all without stint to good and evil alike, who is not troubled by insults, always remaining in His own perfect goodness which does not visualize itself in contrast to evil.

Beginners (*servi*) must start with fear. Proficients (*mercenarii*) are moved by hope of reward. The Perfect (*filii*) believing that all which belongs to their Father belongs to them, are perfected in the image and likeness of God. Here we love God as He has loved us. Just as He has saved us out of pure love for us, so we receive His grace out of pure love for Him. He uses expressions which are basic in the mystical theology of the Fathers: "through the indissoluble grace of love" (suggesting perfect and inviolable union with God by love); "to receive the image and likeness of the Father" (distinction between image and likeness—perfect likeness, perfect union, perfect charity—pure love without admixture of any other motive). Why this love for love's sake is perfection:

1) It does not depend on the opinions of others, or their favor.

2) It purifies the heart of all interior evil inclinations and thoughts. Where there is perfect love of good for its own sake, all that is contrary to it is detested *summo horrore* "with the greatest horror"—and this not out of fear of punishment or hope of reward, but simply because of the opposition between evil and good.

3) In this case there is more perfect freedom and spontaneity in good. One is not motivated by an outside force, but by the good itself, which has become so to speak part of one's own being.

4) Hence there is perfect stability in the good, and therefore peace.

5) Man is then his own judge (implication that he is no longer in need of a judge). He can judge and guide himself because he is perfectly united with God Who is Love—"Love, and do what you will," says St. Augustine. This must be properly understood.

Cassian says:

> Carrying about his conscience with him everywhere and always, as a witness not only of his acts but also of his thoughts, he strives most intently to please it, which he knows he cannot cheat, nor deceive, nor evade.

> Love of good for God's sake alone, merely to please Him: this is perfection. And this is, in fact, the traditional teaching of the Church and of the saints, down through the ages.

The twelfth Conference is on chastity; it specifically deals with the problem [of] whether it is possible for one to be so perfect in chastity that he can avoid all motions of fleshly concupiscence. Chaeremon says that it is possible, but not by our own efforts. Yet he prescribes great mortifications in order to attain it: fasts, solitude, silence, vigils, etc. This is what leads to the problem that is discussed in the thirteenth Conference, on free will and grace. For Germanus cannot understand how it is possible that man should have to make so many efforts, and yet the victory should be attributed to God's grace.

It is to be noticed that the error on free will and grace comes in this context—the struggle for "perfect" chastity, which preoccupied the Desert Fathers. This should teach us to avoid their extremism. It is for us, with St. Paul, to learn the lesson that God's grace is sufficient, and that holiness demands the acceptance of our human frailty and the willingness to face trial with patience. This is a way of realism and of humility.

Abbot Pinufius

Pinufius was an old friend of Cassian and Germanus. In the days when they had shared a cell (hut) together at Bethlehem, Pinufius had run away from Egypt because, having been ordained and appointed abbot of a great cenobium, "he thought that he was already receiving his reward in the human praise of his virtues that was spread far and wide." Fearing thus to lose his eternal reward, he fled first to Tabenna, preferring to conceal himself in the great community rather than live as a solitary in the desert. He presented himself as a postulant in secular clothes and spent many days "in tears" at the gate, throwing himself at the feet of all and asking their prayers. Having been admitted to be tried, he was placed under obedience to a young monk—spent three years here in great humility and obedience, but was recognized. Pinufius attributed this discovery to the devil, and escaped again, this time taking ship to Palestine where he lived with Cassian and Germanus.

In the fourth book of the *Instituta*, Cassian reports an address given by Pinufius to a novice making profession in his monastery at Panephysis. It is a summary (*breviarium*) of the whole way of monastic perfection. Pinufius first of all stresses that renunciation is essential to the monastic state. The monk lives under the sign of the cross. By his renunciation, Christ lives in him. The monastic life is a continual carrying of the Cross. And the Cross of the monk is spiritual, the fear of the Lord which restrains his desires and his own will. Then come the following points:

1) The beginning of salvation and wisdom is the fear of the Lord;

2) This brings forth compunction of heart;

3) Which leads us to strip ourselves of everything for love of God;

4) This in turn brings about humility;

5) When we are humble, then we mortify our wills;

6) This enables us to get free from vice and practice virtue;

7) This leads to purity of heart which is the perfection of charity.

"The perfection of Apostolic love is gained through purity of heart."

The two visitors are very much humbled by all this, and imagining themselves to be at the bottom of the ladder, ask Pinufius to tell them what at least is true compunction so that they can climb the first step. Pinufius praises their humility, tells them they are well advanced, and gives a conference (Conf. 20) on how long one must do penance to satisfy for one's sins. The answer, in brief, is "until they are completely forgotten"—that is to say until we no longer suffer any temptation or experience any phantasms proceeding from that kind of sin. Should we deliberately call to mind the shame of past sins? Yes, he says, except in the case of sins of the flesh, for "as long as one bends over a sewer and stirs up the filth, one will inevitably be suffocated by the evil smell."

The Desert of Scete—and Nitria

West of the Nile, near the coast, between the desert of Scete and Nitria, in the uplands, was the desert of the "cells," famous place of more solitary hermitages. Palladius said there were about 5,000 monks living on the mountain at Nitria, some alone, some in twos. A big church, a common bakery supplies all the monks. Nitria was the first foundation of Abbot Macarius.

Cassian was very eager to get to Scete, the "home of all perfect living." He found there four churches, therefore four congregations of hermits, each one directed by a priest. Scete is the home of the most experienced and tried hermits: "the most tested fathers." It is the place where the most erudite and illuminated of the contemplatives are to be found; "they surpassed in perfection and in knowledge all who were in the monasteries of Egypt." (Conf. 10:2). Cassian spent most of his first seven years here and returned after his visit to Bethlehem for seven years more. The most important of the conferences are those which he based on the teachings of the Fathers at Scete.

Scete was a center of monastic wisdom; here were collected and written the *Verba Seniorum* (*Apothegmata*), "Sayings" of the great Desert Fathers from St. Anthony to Arsenius. These were the words of men taught by the Spirit of God. They consist of:

a) Sentences, or "words of salvation" (proverbs);

b) Anecdotes: stories of the Fathers, illustrating a point;

c) Parables: stories of symbolic deeds, or allegorical sayings.

The great theme of all these *Verba* is salvation. When the Desert Fathers met one another, their greeting was "*sotheies*" ("Mayest thou be saved"). They travelled together a way of salvation that began with flight from the world.

The monastic life is the work of God, having three divisions: solitude, work, and prayer. Their aim was peace, liberty of spirit, purity of heart, freedom from all desires, living with God alone, like Bessarion who lived "without any more cares than a bird in the heavens . . . no house, no desire to go anywhere, . . . no books, entirely freed from all bodily desires . . . living only on the hope of eternal bliss, resting only in the firmness of his faith . . . going hither and thither persevering in nakedness and cold, or scorched by the fires of the sun, stopping in gorges like a strayed traveller or wandering over the far stretching desert as if over the ocean." This picture of a desert wanderer is idyllic, but represents something of the ideal of the Fathers (except that most of them favored a strict stability in the cell!). Some had disciples, others lived in strict solitude, like Arsenius, thirty-two miles from the nearest cell. About the same time that Cassian visited Scete, or a little later, Palladius also came there. He after-wards wrote the *Historia Lausiaca*. A few years later, in 395, seven monks of Jerusalem visited the whole of Egypt from south to north and their experiences were described in the *Historia Monachorum*.

The hermitage of Scete had been founded by St. Macarius about 330. He died about 390 and was still alive when Cassian visited the desert. Cassian refers to him as the "Great Man." Cassian probably visited Evagrius Ponticus also in the Desert of Scete. Cassian writes nothing of the teaching of these great men, but he has left us portraits of others, upon whose teaching he bases his conferences:

1—Paphnutius "The Buffalo": He was the priest of Scete. Cassian speaks of Scete as "our monastery" which means he was admitted there for a time as a monk. Paphnutius lived in a cell five miles from the Church, and would not change to a closer one in spite of his great age. He had no spring nearby and had to carry a week's supply of water when he came back after Mass on Sunday. He would not let a younger brother do this for him. He did this for ninety years. After a brief formation in the ceno-bium he had hastened to the desert out of love of contemplation. He soon learned to hide himself so well that even the most ex-perienced could not find him, and consequently he received the name of "buffalo" because he could, like that animal, hide himself in the wilderness.

Paphnutius gives the third Conference on the "Three Renun-ciations." This deals with "three kinds of vocation": 1) In which one is called directly by God, as was St. Anthony; 2) In which one is inspired by the example of holy souls, or by their teaching; 3) In which one is driven by necessity, by fear of death, or of damnation, by the loss of dear ones or of money, etc. Even though this third is the weakest kind of vocation, it has resulted in men becoming great saints.

After the three vocations, he goes on to the three renuncia-tions: 1) Giving up all our possessions; 2) Giving up our former habits and way of life; 3) Turning our minds away from all that is passing, and living for eternal goods.

2—*Abbot Daniel*: gives the fourth *Conference* on the struggle between flesh and spirit. He was Paphnutius's deacon. Equal to the others in virtue, he outshone them by his humility, and because of this had been chosen deacon. Paphnutius planned that Daniel should succeed him as the priest of Scete. Indeed, he was ordained priest, but never exercised any other function than that of deacon as long as Paphnutius was alive. In the end, Daniel died before Paphnutius and never got to exercise his priestly order. The conference on the conflict between flesh and spirit is really about distractions and trials that make the interior life difficult.

3—*Abbot Serenus*: They are invited to a "banquet" with this Desert Father ("a most sumptuous repast"—Conf. 8). The "banquet" of Abbot Serenus consisted of bread, dipped in sauce, salt; three olives each; five chick peas. "To eat more would be a sin in the desert." (Ordinary regime—2 lbs. of bread daily, of which some might be set aside for guests.) Abbot Serenus is eminent for his chastity, never troubled at all by the flesh even in sleep. He had worked for this by prayers day and night and fasts and vigils.

He gives Conference 7 on distractions and the temptations of the devil, and 8 on the different orders of angelic spirits. Conference 7 stresses the importance of controlling one's thoughts, which requires effort and "great sorrow of heart." We have the grace of God to help us reject all evil thoughts. Devils cannot force the inmost sanctuary of the will, but can only tell how their suggestions are received by observing outward signs.

4—*Abbot Theonas*: who had been married, according to the desire of his parents, while still young, had brought gifts as a layman to Abbot John. The latter had addressed to him a strong exhortation, saying "if you give away the tithes of your goods, you are fulfilling the perfection of the Old Law. But if you seek evangelical perfection, you must give away all that you have and follow Christ." Theonas tries to persuade his wife to leave the world so that he also can become a monk, and when she refuses, he believes himself inspired by God to run away to the desert anyway. Cassian hastens to say this is not a general rule, but that it was justified in this particular case. Theonas gives them three conferences. The first (Conf. 21) is on the lack of fasting during Paschal Time. Cassian is curious to know why the monks of Egypt are so careful not to fast in Paschal Time, and why they pray standing up, and avoid kneeling during that season while so many in Syria continued fasting etc.

The second conference of Theonas is on Nocturnal Illusions (Conf. 22). It was given in response to the question why those who fast are often more tempted by the lust of the flesh than others who keep a less strict fast. He offers three explanations: 1) Perhaps gluttony of the past has an influence; 2) Perhaps the soul has not guarded purity of heart; 3) The envy of the devil tries to disturb souls who are striving to be fervent. A modern observer might add another answer—somewhat akin to this third, that the trouble might be caused by nervous and mental strain. Those who give themselves to asceticism with inordinate tension must expect their systems to take its revenge.

This leads into the next conference of Theonas (Conf. 23)— "On Willing Good and Doing Evil." The problem is raised by St. Paul in Romans 7, "It is not what I wish that I do, but what I hate that I do . . ." etc. (vss. 15-25). This text has been much misused by heretics. Theonas begins by making it clear that this does not apply to deliberate sins. The words are spoken by St. Paul, who was a saint and full of every virtue. The "good" that he desires and which he cannot have at will must be something higher than virtue. It is *theoria*, the perfect purity of heart which belongs to pure charity and contemplation. The goodness he aspires to is the goodness of God dwelling in us, by comparison with which goodness our virtues are as filthy rags (Isa. 64). The purity he aspires to is that of the Gospel, compared with which the virtues of the Law are as nothing. The burden Theonas complains of is the burden of a self laden with illusion and falsity due to original sin—often even our good intentions are full of hidden evil. The souls to be pitied are not the ones who feel this—it is a salutary suffering, but the souls that cannot feel it and think everything is perfect with them. At the same time we must not be pushed into discouragement and sadness. So in these words, according to Theonas, Paul is saying that in spite of all his efforts and virtues, he laments the fact that he cannot always contemplate God in purity of heart, but is troubled and disturbed by his nature, in temptations, trials and indeliberate or semi-deliberate sins.

The problem of this Conference is, in fact, the problem of distractions, and of indeliberate weakness and faults. The saints, Theonas reminds us, have a very acute sense of sin and suffer much from these imperfections. But the view of their miseries produces in them true humility. They realize that they cannot do the impossible, that they will undoubtedly be left with their faults and sins until the end of their days, but for the grace of God which alone can deliver them from "the body of this death." Hence, accepting their faults, their limitations, in true humility, they rely no more on their own powers but prostrate themselves before God in humble prayer. Hence they eat their "spiritual bread" (which is Christ) in the sweat of their brow. And thus they share the common lot of men. They must truly recognize themselves as sinners, like the rest of men. In a beautiful eucharistic passage which closes the conference, Theonas reproves the presumption of those who only communicate once a year, with the implication that communion is only for those who are most pure and perfect saints. Hence they believe themselves worthy, once a year. But it is much better to receive the Lord each Sunday conscious of our needs and miseries, going to Communion as to the necessary medicine for our frailties. Hence, here too we see great emphasis on humility, on trust in God's mercy, and above all on love for the Blessed Eucharist, the source of sanctity. This is important because it is something often overlooked in the spirituality of the Desert Fathers.

Other Fathers, about whom Cassian gives us fewer details, are Abbot Moses, Abbot Isaac, Abbot Abraham, on mortification; also Abbot Theodore, who lives in the desert of the Cells, [a] plateau between Nitria and Scete, who discusses with them the problem of the death of the Palestinian hermits, killed in the desert of Juda by Saracens. His reply is that there is no problem if living by faith, we have the true idea of good and evil. Death is no evil to the Christian, since Christ has overcome death. What is good, is to do the will of God. What is evil is to disobey God. In between come things that are neither absolutely good or evil in themselves, and whose value depends on how we use them. Life and death are among these. In this conference (Conf. 6) he also takes up other questions, such as stability, temptations, the value of trials, and making good use of suffering and temptation.

The Origenist Conflict

During the time of Cassian's journey to Egypt, the Origenist conflict arose. It is important in the history of monastic spirituality for it marks the end of the great age of Egyptian monasticism. Origenism, as condemned by the Church, consists chiefly of errors flowing from Origen's teaching on the preexistence of souls—and the *apocatastasis* (or a final settlement when all, even the damned, return to God); also his Trinitarian errors. In 393, Palestinian monks—the severe ones—start a great storm over Origen. They present themselves at the cell of St. Jerome and demand that Origen be condemned. St. Jerome repudiated all taint of Origenist teaching in his own writings, though retaining great respect for Origen. Jerome's friend Rufinus refused to sign up with the attackers of Origen. Then Epiphanius of Salamina came to Jerusalem, and thinking he detected Origenist opinions in the talk of the Bishop of Jerusalem, had a violent argument with him, and went off to St. Jerome, who broke with the Bishop of Jerusalem. Rufinus, Jerome's friend, on the contrary sided with the bishop. Bitter conflict between Rufinus and Jerome then developed.

The fight spread to Egypt, where the Doctors had hitherto been content to pass over Origen's errors in silence, while highlighting the truths taught by him. Among their number was St. Athanasius. But when the conflict arose, it divided the contemplatives: students of Scripture who naturally loved Origen, headed by Evagrius Ponticus, against the actives who distrusted lofty doctrines which they did not understand and who were looking for an opportunity to get the contemplatives condemned. Some of the monks met by Cassian were of this last party, especially Abbot Abraham, who thinks the reading of Scripture is of little value. The actives, however, had fallen into another heresy, *anthropomorphism*, believing that God had the form of a man, not only in the Incarnation but in His own being.

In 399, after the death of Evagrius, Archbishop Theophilus of Alexandria, an Origenist who wants to gain control over the desert, sends his paschal letter (announcing the feast—cf. announcement of Easter in our chapter rooms today) and included a condemnation of anthropomorphism to please Origenist monks. Three congregations of Scete declared the bishop heretical and refused to read the pastoral letter. Paphnutius alone held firm. See the story of old Abbot Serapion, who cannot give up the heresy, until finally convinced by a learned visitor from Cappadocia, he sobs, "They have taken away my God." (Conf. 10)

Rioting monks in Alexandria persuaded Theophilus to condemn Origen. He meets them saying, "When I see you, I see the face of God." They reply, "If you believe that, condemn Origen." Thus they got some satisfaction. Having changed his position completely, Theophilus now begins a persecution of the Origenists in the desert, supported by the actives. The Origenists begin to leave Egypt, either expelled, or departing of their own accord. Theophilus (according to Palladius, pro-Origen) attacked Nitria with soldiers, burnt three cells, books, etc. Theophilus in turn said Origenists fortified Nitria to resist his "visitation."

Isidore and the "Tall Brothers" (four leading Origenists) lead a troop of three hundred Origenist exiles to Palestine. Leaders go on to Constantinople, to get support of St. Chrysostom.

Was Cassian involved in the Origenist conflict? He himself says nothing directly about his own part. [There is] no Origenist heresy in Cassian, but Cassian follows Evagrius, in orthodox Origenist ascetic doctrine. Cassian probably knew Evagrius. Cassian's friends (Paphnutius, etc.) were the Origenists of Nitria. [Also], Cassian leaves Egypt at this time and is found at Constantinople where he is ordained around 402.

It is probable that Cassian and Germanus left Egypt with the Origenists, or as a result of the struggle. They were probably involved with the Origenist theologians and probably rated as the frowned on "foreign element" which Theophilus and the Copts attacked at Nitria (out of political opportunism of course). The golden age of Egyptian monasticism came to its end at the moment when Cassian left Egypt, at the beginning of the fifth century. Now the monastic movement would gain firm foothold in the West, especially in Southern France.

Constantinople and Gaul

The Origenists fled to Chrysostom because he was an ardent and uncompromising defender of the truth—not a politician or an opportunist. Indeed he was not enough of a diplomat for some: too outspoken; no human respect; above petty squabbles—a holy and objective thinker. Cassian was an enthusiastic admirer of Chrysostom, who ordained him deacon.

St. John Chrysostom was born in 347 at Antioch. He was a great orator at Antioch who pleads the cause of the poor. In 398 he was consecrated archbishop of Constantinople and shows ardent reforming zeal along with fearless condemnation of abuses. Cassian considered Chrysostom an ideal bishop and a great saint. He pointed to him as a master. However there is apparently little real influence of Chrysostom in Cassian. (He quotes him once only and the sentence has never been found in Chrysostom's writings!)

From Constantinople, Cassian went to Rome where he met and made friends with St. Leo the Great, not yet Pope. (Some think he met Pelagius at Rome at this time.) Legend says that in his contact with Cassian, St. Leo wanted to go off and be a hermit but was forbidden by Pope Innocent I. In 410, Alaric and the Goths invade Italy. Cassian leaves about this time. He goes to Marseilles, where the bishop is a friend of St. Jerome and St. Honoratus and a patron of the monastic movement. Cassian was ordained priest by Innocent I or Proculus, Bishop of Marseilles.

Provence was the last refuge of Roman and Christian civilization as the barbarians broke through in the north and in Italy. Refugees came from France and Italy. Many of these refugees, disillusioned with the world, became monks. In 412, Visigoths passed through Provence and unsuccessfully besieged Marseilles. Arles became capital of Gaul. Monasticism existed in Gaul (St. Martin, St. Honoratus, etc.) but it was still not completely accepted even by Christians. Bishops persecuted the monks, crowds mocked and attacked them. In many places, monks were accused of heresy, and Proculus of Marseilles did not have an easy time of it because he liked the monks. His adversaries used this as a weapon against him. Gallic monasticism was also still internally weak.

Cassian was admirably fitted to make the great synthesis of monastic doctrine and adapt the Eastern tradition to the West:

1) He was an experienced monk himself;

2) He had met and lived with the greatest monks of his time;

3) He knew all the great centers of monasticism;

4) He knew both the cenobites and the hermits;

5) He was steeped in monastic doctrine;

6) He himself had a high monastic ideal;

7) He had the genius required to make this synthesis.

Cassian arrived at Marseilles about 410. The monastery of Lérins had just been founded. Cassian founds the monastery of St. Victor, on a point across the bay from the city—a center for monastic life in southern France. Castor, Bishop of Apt (back in the mountains) asks for some writings on monasticism and Cassian writes the *Instituta* (about 420). The idea was to give a basis for uniform observance based on the traditions of the East. The *Conferences* were written 425–428. The influence of his writings dominated Lérins—nursery of bishops, who soon took over great dioceses of France. This influence spreads through Italy, Spain, Africa. His influence on St. Benedict made him, in fact, a permanent force in Western monasticism. He died about 433, shortly after being attacked as a semi-pelagian. [His] local cult grew—with [a] feast at Marseilles on July 23—Pope Urban V engraved the words "Sanctus Cassianus" on a silver casket containing his relics. The Oriental Church still celebrates his Feast on February 29. In the *Philokalia* he is included as Saint Cassian the Roman.

The Conferences of Cassian

here are twenty-four conferences. This whole group is divided into three parts. Part I consists of ten conferences of hermits in Scete: Abba Moses on the essence of the Monastic Life and on Discretion; Abba Paphnutius on the Triple Renunciation; Abba Daniel on concupiscence and conflict of flesh and spirit; Abba Serapion on the Eight Principal Vices (cf. *Instituta*); Abba Theodorus on why God permits the saints to be killed; Abba Serenus: two on Distractions, Devils and Temptations; Abba Isaac: two on prayer. This part contains the best and most important of the conferences and we will do well to concentrate on these.

The Prologue to the First Part is addressed to Bishop Leontius and to "Brother Helladius" (the latter evidently a hermit in France). Cassian, writing in retirement in his monastery ("in the harbor of silence"), will look out upon the "vast sea" of doctrine of these Fathers of Scete, awed by the fact that here is the wisdom of great solitaries and contemplatives, elevated far above the *anachoresis* of cenobites. The difference between the *Instituta* (for cenobites) and the *Conferences* (for hermits) lies in the fact that the *Instituta* deal with observances, liturgy and asceticism, the *Conferences* with "the invisible state (*habitus*) of the interior man," with perpetual prayer and contemplation. He warns the reader not to be upset at the loftiness and difficulty of the ideals proposed and not to judge them by his own state and vocation (presumably if he is a cenobite) because he does not have the wherewithal to make a right judgement. One cannot fully appreciate these doctrines, says Cassian, unless one has lived in the desert and experienced the illumination of mind which comes from dwelling alone in the vast emptiness of total solitude.

Undoubtedly the first two conferences are among the most important of all Cassian's writings. They are absolutely fundamental and without a knowledge of his doctrine on purity of heart and discretion, we would fail to understand the true monastic attitude and miss the whole purpose of the monastic life. They show us that contemplation does not consist exclusively in solitude and silence and renunciation but that these are only means to purity of heart. Aspirations to a "more perfect life" are to be interpreted by us as inspirations to seek a greater interior perfection.

Conference 1: "On the Purpose and Goal of the Monk"

What is the purpose and end of the monastic life? This is the great and all-important question to which we must always return. Why have we left the world? The answer is given by Abbot Moses, a hermit of Scete. "We have come to the desert, he says, to seek the Kingdom of God, and the way to enter the Kingdom is by achieving purity of heart." To begin with, Cassian shows us the modesty of Abbot Moses, and his great hesitation to embark on a spiritual discourse. The Desert Fathers lived in the true spirit of silence, and were not given to much talking, or indiscriminate talking even about spiritual things. Hence Moses has to be begged "with tears" to tell them something. It would be wrong to reveal the secrets of the spiritual life to the curious or the indifferent.

What is the purpose of the monastic life? The *skopos* and the *telos*—the immediate objective and the final end. This distinction must be made first of all. The monastic life, being an "art," has these two distinct aims: one immediate, the other ultimate.

When the farmer clears the ground and ploughs, it is to prepare it for seeding: this preparation is the *skopos*. The *telos* is the harvest. In the monastic life we have a *skopos* and a *telos*, and for these we undergo all our labors and hardships. We know what we seek, and this is sufficient to make every sacrifice worthwhile. If you do not know what you are after, it is much harder, in fact almost impossible, to apply yourself to the search.

Moses asks them why they have undertaken their long journey and their sojourn in the desert. They answer, "For the Kingdom of God" and this he says is the right answer; this is the *telos*. But what is the immediate objective—the *skopos*? Note the practical importance of this. In order to act prudently we must take into account not only what is general and universal, but above all what is particular and concrete. I must not only do "good" in a big, general way, but there is a particular good that must be done here and now. If I do not see it, I will not act rightly. Hence the importance of having a clear immediate aim even in small things: to know what we are doing, not confine ourselves to big universal aims; in the particular case their power to move us may be very weak, for example in meditation, [for which it is] better to have a precise aim, not just "union with God."

Cassian and Germanus confess that they do not know what is the immediate objective of the monastic life and many monks today are in the same predicament. Hence Abbot Moses says definitely: "In every art and discipline a particular target is paramount: that is, an end point for the soul, a constant intention for the mind, for no one will be able to reach the objective of a desired goal unless he keeps this target in focus with complete attentiveness and perseverance." The *skopos* has a certain primacy, hence importance.

It must be seen and kept in mind with perseverance and care. It is the "intention of the mind"—the what and the how and the why of our conduct. Without it, our activity is wasted and gets nowhere. "Those who proceed without a road to follow have labor and not advantage for their journey."

The *skopos* is purity of heart. "Indeed our aim, that is, the target, is purity of heart, without which it is impossible for anyone to reach the ultimate goal." Hence, if we are to make a success of the monastic life, we must turn all our attention and all our efforts to gaining purity of heart, that is the ability to love God purely and to do His will for love's sake alone: disinterested love. This apparently simple little principle, which we all take more or less for granted once we hear it, is one that has had a profound effect on all monastic spirituality. St. Benedict is based on it, and St. Bernard's mystical theology is built on it as on a cornerstone.

Hence, a second practical principle of great importance: "Therefore whatever can direct us toward this target, that is, purity of heart, should be followed with absolute commitment; but whatever pulls us away from it, should be shunned as dangerous and poisonous." What is good for us? Everything that helps us gain purity of heart. What is bad for us? Everything that prevents us from purifying our hearts. "For this we do and suffer all, for this we have left our families, our dignities, riches, pleasures," etc.

Applications and illustrations:

1) It is useless to leave great riches in the world and become attached to a pen or a needle in the desert: the heart is not pure, because the monk has not kept his objective in view. His eye has wandered and become ensnared by a trifling possession (this then has become his *skopos*). He speaks of one being so attached to a book that he will not even let another touch it or look at it. We remember that a regular war was precipitated among the early Irish monks over a psalter.

2) But purity of heart is equated with perfect charity. "If I should give my goods to feed the poor and have not charity . . . it profiteth me nothing." Hence, purity of heart is not the mere external act of renunciation and emptying one's hands. The heart must be emptied of love for creatures and open itself entirely to the love of God. Hence, further important details: purity of heart

means—no jealousy, no vanity, no pride, no rivalry, anger, self-ishness, no rejoicing in the evil that befalls others, not thinking evil thoughts of them; all this is to offer a pure heart to God. It is the ideal of *apatheia* (freedom from passion), the crown of the "active life."

3) It is for the sake of purity of heart that we do everything we do in the monastic life. Each monastic observance, fasting, silence, reading, labor, etc., has as its function to purify the heart of vices and self-love, to free it from passion, and to raise us to the perfection of charity, "to make ready our heart, unharmed by all noxious passions, . . . by depending on these steps to rise to the perfection of love."

4) If on the other hand, we fall into sadness or disquiet when we have to omit one or other of these observances for the sake of something higher (for example—to forego fasting in order to entertain a guest) then it shows that the observance is not serving its purpose. For the very purpose of these observances is to purify our souls of anger and sadness and the other vices.

5) It must be understood that if our observances are not working for purity of heart then they will work against it (that is, if we are attached to them out of motives of self-love). "The profit of fasting is not as great as the loss we suffer through anger, and the fruit we gather through reading is less than the harm we incur through despising a brother."

He clearly states the great distinction between ends and means. Fasting, etc., are means, *instrumenta*. Charity is the end. Perfection does not lie in the means, but in the end attained by them. This cardinal principle of the monastic life must never be forgotten. If we remember it, we should logically make a generous and perfect use of the means, and thus attain our end. If we forget it, we will inevitably waste our efforts and our monastic life will end in frustration, even perhaps in sheer illusion. "One who is satisfied with (the means) as if they were the chief good, and limits the strivings of his heart to this alone and does not apply all his energies to achieving the end . . . will undertake all these exercises fruitlessly."

Peace, tranquility, purity of heart in perfect love, this is the summit of the monastic life: it is the life of contemplation, which the monk leads alone with God. Here Cassian simply repeats what has been said, and makes clear that contemplative life on earth is the *skopos* which we must seek by active asceticism. Cassian says:

> Therefore this should be our main effort, this unwavering purpose should be unceasingly aspired to: that our mind always cling to God and to divine things.

[Then, he] adds: "Whatever differs from this, however great it may be, is to be rated as secondary, or indeed as trifling if not actually harmful." He then goes on to speak of Martha and Mary in the Gospel (Luke 10). In Cassian's use of the story, Martha represents the active life in the ancient sense of the practice of virtue, the *bios praktikos*, which leads to *apatheia*, and thence to *theoria* (contemplation). He is not at all speaking of the apostolic life or preaching as contrasted with the enclosed life of the monk. The works of Martha, practicing the virtues and following out the observances which form us to the life of virtue, is indeed not a "*vile opus*" ("a worthless work") but a "*laudabile ministerium*" ("praiseworthy ministry").

All the Desert Fathers agree that there is also an illusory "active life" or a temptation to activism in which the monk indulges in unnecessary activity (trumped up with false pretexts) in order to avoid being alone with himself before God.

Conference 2: "On Discretion"

At the end of the first Conference, Abbot Moses observes that they have passed naturally from purity of heart to a new subject: discretion. He adds that they have now been up late and

talked long. Hence he will break off, and they can get the necessary sleep to refresh body and mind, so that on the next day he
may speak to them of discretion after they have first practiced
it by moderation in speech and taking the necessary rest. He
tells them that the subject of discretion is very important, since
according to him discretion holds the first place among the virtues. (This can be held in the sense in which St. Thomas holds
that prudence: [a] disposes the use of means towards attaining
the proper end of each moral virtue; [b] by disposing the means
properly, it aids us in attaining the proper balance between extremes, which is essential to every moral virtue [II–II, Q. 47, art.
6 and 7]. Hence without prudence the other moral virtues will
not function properly, and in this sense prudence is the most
important of them all.) Cassian's discretion is a special aspect
of prudence: prudence in so far as it is enlightened as to the true
motives of our actions, and disposes means to ends in the light
of this knowledge. But it is also more than prudence, it is a work
of the Gift of Counsel.

Chapter 1: Abbot Moses begins by stating that the necessity
of discretion will be seen from the examples of the many Desert
Fathers who fell through lack of it. And this is the sober truth.
He will therefore concentrate first on the need for discretion.
Then he will go on to discuss the ways of acquiring and practic-
ing it.

Moses declares that discretion is a heroic virtue, "not an
ordinary virtue." He adds that it is eminently supernatural, and
a true gift of grace, "not one which human effort is somehow
capable of gaining, unless it has been united with the divine gift
of grace." Here he speaks evidently not only of the infused virtue
of prudence but of the charismatic gift of discernment of spirits.
Scholastic theology would make clearer distinctions. It is for us
to take Cassian as he stands, and not to demand too great technical precision: "The task assigned to discretion is neither earthly
nor small. . . . The monk must go after it with all his energies."
Note his description of discretion as a certain knowledge of the

"spirits that arise within us." "If not, he will walk in complete darkness, and not only incur grave dangers of complete spiritual ruin, but meet with many obstacles and difficulties where the way should be smooth and simple."

[For] proof from the tradition of the Desert Fathers, especially St. Anthony, read an account of a discussion of St. Anthony and his disciples at which Moses was present as a young monk in the Thebaid. The question was raised, which is the most important of the virtues (or means of monastic perfection)? Some said fasting, vigils; others poverty, solitude; still others, in the practice of fraternal charity. St. Anthony having listened to them all, said: "All these things are necessary and useful—but many who have practiced them have nevertheless come to ruin. Hence they do not of themselves bring a monk to sanctity. There must be something else." He adds that if they study the ruin of great ascetics and solitaries and find out what was lacking, they will probably discover the real key to true perfection, "that which first and foremost leads to God." They fell because they went to excess, and they did this because they had not been properly instructed in the ways of monastic perfection and hence lacked discretion. Without discretion their other virtues came to nothing and bore no fruit. Discretion, avoiding contrary extremes, teaches the royal road to God, and this discretion is what the Gospel calls: "the light of the body which is the eye, and if the eye be single the whole body is lightsome" (Matt. 6:23). Discretion is neither carried away by enthusiasm, "lifted up" in time of fervor, nor depressed and discouraged in time of trial. After the discussion of some Scripture texts on the necessity of doing all things with wisdom and counsel Abbot Moses concludes that "no virtue can be made perfect or even continue in existence without discretion." Discretion leads us safely to God; it brings us more easily to the heights of perfection, while without it these heights would be impossible to reach at all by most men. Discretion in a word gives sound judgement which is absolutely necessary in a solitary. It gives solidity and perseverance to monastic vocation: "that leads a monk undisturbed to God by set stages."

Examples of indiscretion: Hero—following his own will and judgement rather than the monastic traditions, [he] refused to participate in Easter synaxis, [and] deluded by the devil, he jumped in a well; the two brothers in the desert, one of whom dies of presumption because he wants to be fed by a miracle; the monk who tried to sacrifice his son to God, deluded after many false visions—his son sees him sharpening up the knife and takes to flight; the monk whose illusory revelations led him to circumcise himself and fall into Judaism. In all these examples we have presumption, independence, reliance on one's own interior lights, leading to complete lack of contact with reality and gross errors ending in spiritual destruction.

Fully convinced by these stories that discretion is absolutely necessary and that all the other virtues depend on it, Germanus asks how it may be acquired and how true and false discretion may be known. Moses answers that discretion depends entirely on humility. (St. Benedict was therefore very wise in making it the heart of his ascesis and of his *Rule*.)

Signs of true humility:

a) The first sign of humility is submission to the judgement of a senior (Spiritual Father), not only in the matter of one's actions but also of all one's judgements. Humility therefore goes with docility, and obedience. It is marked by a salutary distrust of our own judgements, and submission to those who have likewise submitted to those before them. This standard is practical only when applied to concrete monasteries and Spiritual Fathers. It is not merely a matter of guiding yourself with an approved book, but of following the customs and traditions of the group to which you belong. If it is certain that these customs and traditions are not for you, then go elsewhere.

b) Together with docility, the other necessary disposition for acquiring discretion is openness with the Spiritual Father. The enemy cannot deceive one who, "has learned not to conceal, out of a dangerous shame, all the thoughts being produced in his heart, but either rejects or allows them in conformity with the mature probing of the elders." By this we are protected against our own ignorance and inexperience. Evil or indiscreet thoughts often lose their sting as soon as we resolve to manifest them.

[Consider] the example of the disciple who was hiding an extra loaf and eating it in the evening—the devil departs from him as soon as he confesses his fault to the Spiritual Father. Conclusion: the devil ruins those who trust in their own judgement and hide their acts and thoughts from their Spiritual Father.

[Now,] not all Spiritual Fathers are of equal merit. Cassian does not believe blindly in manifestation of conscience as a universal remedy for all ills. It can happen that the Father himself is indiscreet. Hence one must make a wise choice of the senior to whom one entrusts himself. The mere fact that a monk is old and has grey hair does not mean that we should accept his teaching or follow his example. The Spiritual Father himself is to be chosen for his true discretion, proved by a long life of virtue, and by fidelity to the true monastic tradition, not just adherence to his own will and opinions. The prudent Father is one who is able to understand and [is] compassionate with human weakness. He must above all understand that it is grace of God that makes saints.

The second Conference ends with answering the main question which had interested Germanus and Cassian, namely how to overcome distractions and live in a state of continual prayer. This will be treated in Conferences 9 and 10 by Abbot Isaac; also in Conference 4 of Abbot Daniel, on Temptations, and Conference 7 of Abbot Serenus, on "The Instability of the Mind and Evil Spirits."

Conference 4:
"On the Desire of the Flesh and of the Spirit"
by Abbot Daniel

The question: Why are our thoughts and moods so mobile and unstable? Consolation and desolation—fervor and inability to pray—alternate without apparent reason.

> We asked this blessed Daniel why it was that as we sat in the cells we were sometimes filled with the utmost gladness of heart, together with inexpressible delight and abundance of the holiest feelings, so that I will not say speech, but even feeling could not follow it, and pure prayers were readily breathed, and the mind being filled with spiritual fruits, praying to God even in sleep could feel that its petitions rose lightly and powerfully to God: and again, why it was that for no reason we were suddenly filled with the utmost grief, and weighed down with unreasonable depression, so that we not only felt as if we ourselves were overcome with such feelings, but also our cell grew dreadful, reading palled upon us, aye and our very prayers were offered up unsteadily and vaguely, and almost as if we were intoxicated: so that while we were groaning and endeavoring to restore ourselves to our former disposition, our mind was unable to do this, and the more earnestly it sought to fix again its gaze upon God, so was it the more vehemently carried away to wandering thoughts by shifting aberrations and so utterly deprived of all spiritual fruits, as not to be capable of being roused from this deadly slumber even by the desire of the kingdom of heaven, or by the fear of hell held out to it.

Threefold cause: "from our own negligence, or from the attack of the devil, or from the permission of the Lord." He begins with this one.

Reasons for our testing by Divine action causing aridity and desolation.

1) To promote humility and self-knowledge, self-distrust, [and] realization of our dependence on grace.

2) To test our perseverance [and] the seriousness of our will to serve God, and to stimulate us to further effort.

We can do nothing without grace, and indeed grace visits us frequently and awakens us from negligence when we have done nothing to deserve it:

> And by this it is clearly shown that God's grace and mercy always work in us what is good, and that when it forsakes us, the efforts of the worker are useless, and that however earnestly a man may strive, he cannot regain his former condition without His help, and that this saying is constantly fulfilled in our case: that it is "not of him that willeth or runneth but of God which hath mercy." And this grace on the other hand sometimes does not refuse to visit with that holy inspiration of which you spoke, and with an abundance of spiritual thoughts, even the careless and indifferent; but inspires the unworthy, arouses the slumberers, and enlightens those who are blinded by ignorance, and mercifully reproves us and chastens us, shedding itself abroad in our hearts, that thus we may be stirred by the compunction which He excites, and impelled to rise from the sleep of sloth. Lastly we are often filled by His sudden visitation with sweet odours, beyond the power of human composition, so that the soul is ravished with these delights, and caught up, as it were, into an ecstasy of spirit, and becomes oblivious of the fact that it is still in the flesh.

The value of trial and temptation [is then] illustrated by texts from Old and New Testaments. The struggle between flesh and spirit is salutary, willed for us by God to keep us from a false security and complacent self-satisfaction.

[The] psychology of temptation and conflict: in examination of the limits of voluntary control, and involuntary activity of the passions, he represents the will as situated in between "the desire of the flesh" and the "desire of the spirit." The latter a desire and appetite for fasting, prayer, etc. The will is represented as by nature inclined to compromise, wanting the fruits of the spirit without renouncing the flesh; hence, [it is] tepid. However there is another aspect. The will is also inclined to moderation and should not be drawn away to excess even in the use of spiritual means like fasting and mortification. So the struggle is productive of "balance through moderation." The desires of the flesh remind the will to turn to God for help. Excess of mortification leads to exhaustion and will returns to necessary relaxation of flesh in order to maintain a just equilibrium. In this way purity of heart is acquired by constant struggle. Thus the soldier of Christ is taught to follow the "Royal Way," the King's highway (*via regia*) which is the middle path. Demons try to upset this balance by undue pressure on one side or the other—leading to excess in material things or in spiritual exercises.

Conferences 9 and 10: "Abbot Isaac on Prayer"

Together with the first, of which they are a logical continuation, these are the two most important of Cassian's conferences, and the most interesting for contemplative monks. They are the solid foundation of Benedictine prayer.

At the end of Abbot Moses' first Conference on Purity of Heart, the question of distractions and constant prayer was raised. That led into the topic of discretion in the second Conference, but this was a by-path. Not until the ninth Conference does Cassian return to the question of the pure prayer which must constantly rise from the heart of the monk who is tranquil and purified of his attachments to inordinate passion. Conference 9 begins with a résumé of the basic ideas in Conference 1, to tie in the subject of pure prayer. It starts with a treatment of the qualities of pure prayer, goes on to talk of the different kinds of prayer and how they are to be used. This is followed by a brief commentary on the Lord's Prayer. After this, Cassian goes on to speak of mystical prayer and the gift of tears, and returns after that to certain external conditions for solitary prayer.

Conference 10 begins with a couple of brief digressions, on the Egyptian custom for the celebration of Easter and on the anthropomorphite heresy, which leads in to the question of the humanity of Our Lord and our prayer. The rest of the conference is taken up with the question of perpetual prayer and how to avoid distractions. We have already touched upon this in connection with the subject of distractions in the first conference. Let us turn now to Conference 9 which is the more important of the two.

Purity of Heart and Pure Prayer

Abbot Isaac takes up the theme of Abbot Moses: purity of heart. Why? Because the monk is essentially and above all a man of prayer. He purifies his heart in order by prayer and contemplation to be as constantly united with God as is possible in the present life. According to Abbot Isaac, constant prayer is the reason for our withdrawal from the world, and it is the normal accompaniment of purity of heart. The two go together. So just as everything in the monastic life tends to produce purity of heart so everything in the monastic life tends to promote uninterrupted perseverance in prayer, unshaken tranquillity of mind, and perfect purity of heart. With constant prayer there is the problem: not constant consolation; not constant feeling after prayer; prayer as a virtue, a *habitus*, part of a whole context of virtues. All the virtues of the monk tend to this summit of prayer, but if they do not attain it, they cannot remain stable themselves. All the monastic observances should tend to keep us in constant prayer; for instance, the balance between bodily and spiritual works is designed to promote true prayer.

Note the wisdom of the Desert Fathers: A superficial reader of such a text might think the important thing is the perpetual application to prayer and unconsciously think that this would mean perpetual application of the mind in the same way all the time to prayer, and this is in fact fatal to the life of prayer. We must wisely preserve a healthy alternation between bodily and spiritual works, so that our faculties and powers apply themselves in turn in different ways to prayer, and one rests while the other works.

Prayer is the soul of the life of virtue. Prayer is the completion of the edifice of virtue. Virtue without prayer is then imperfect, and the most important thing is lacking to a life of virtue if contemplation (in some sense) is absent from it. Isaac even goes further, and adds that unless the organism of virtue is kept alive and integrated by prayer, which is its fulfillment, it will die and disintegrate. "Unless all these things have been brought together [and joined] with this as its completion, by no means can they endure in firmness and stability." Prayer climaxes and "fixes" perfection. At the same time, prayer (contemplation) cannot be acquired without the exercise of all the virtues. Hence there is a vital and essential relationship between prayer and all the virtues in the spiritual life (virtues—"strengths"). Since the life of prayer is built on the foundation of virtues, it is useless to talk about it unless we keep in mind the virtues on which it depends. This is just another way of linking prayer and purity of heart, because the function of all the virtues is to purify the heart and remove those obstacles which make it difficult or impossible to keep recollected and engage ourselves with God alone.

The most important virtues for the life of prayer, singled out here for special mention, are simplicity, humility, mortification, [and] faith (in the Gospels). When these four foundation stones are laid at the base of the edifice it cannot be shaken by passions or by the attacks of the enemy. But note—it will be attacked. Steps to take in the life of virtue to prepare for pure prayer "in order for prayer to be offered with that fervor and purity that is proper":

a) Get rid of all cares for material things, and for worldly business. A clean sweep must be made of all sources of distraction—i.e., of all avoidable business. Renounce all concern with secular and material affairs, in so far as it is possible.

b) Purify the memory of all vain talk, distractions, idle jokes, and avoid all conversations where these will be heard; hence serious practice of silence.

c) Get rid of temptations to anger, *tristitia* "sadness," and lust—this most of all by solitude, withdrawal from the world.

d) Lay the foundations of humility really deep in the soul ("stable foundations of deep humility").

e) Then build on humility all the other virtues.

f) Take a special care for recollection, outside the time of prayer, lest we bring distractions with us to our prayer. An interesting expression is used: "prostrating ourselves for peace"—for "going to pray" or "settling down to prayer": "peace" taken as synonymous for prayer. Lesson: prayer depends on our submission to God and humility, in which is true peace.

The soul is compared to a feather which, if it is dry, will rise up lightly on the slightest breath of wind, but if it is wet it remains on the ground. So our souls if they are "dry" and pure of all concern with things that are not God, will rise up as it were instinctively, by His grace, to Him. This implies an optimistic view of our souls; they tend spontaneously to God when obstacles are removed, according to Cassian. He speaks of the work of asceticism as restoring the "natural motion" of the soul, by which it seeks God. This is not necessarily Pelagian. He is probably taking grace into account. He does not belong to the age that made clear technical distinctions between nature and grace.

Sources of Distraction

The Lord in the Gospel (Lk. 21:34) does not say that we must take care lest our hearts be weighed down with obvious and terrible sins, like blasphemy, murder, etc., but with surfeiting and drunkenness and the cares of this life. Now, as Abbot Isaac says, the monk is far away from opportunities for reveling and surfeiting, but he warns that there is a kind of spiritual gluttony and drunkenness of which he must beware. This is drunkenness that "does not come from wine" but is as the gall of dragons, a diabolical inebriation that comes from activism. In a word Abbot Isaac is saying that there may not be much chance of surfeiting and drunkenness for the monk, but he can be overwhelmed with cares for temporal things and begin to lose himself entirely in temporalities. The greatest danger to the monk's life of prayer is the possibility of becoming too attached to his work. In order to avoid this attachment, work must be kept strictly to the necessary limits. A monk should mortify the instinct to work overtime or to undertake unnecessary projects. He must see that his jobs do not multiply on all sides. The basic principle: if a monk can support himself on a dollar a day, he should not work for two dollars. The restless soul ruins his life of prayer by constantly imagining there are new things that need to be done. All this is "the passion of worldly desire."

At the other extreme are the monks who do not work at all, or rather who have no zeal for the common work. These, if they do not work for the monastery, are often taken up excessively with projects of their own and it is mere hypocrisy on their part to pretend that they can exempt themselves from the common work in order to "pray." But it is the same disease in both cases: the itch of our human will to work and to produce unnecessarily when we cannot bear the spiritual labor of being alone with God and putting up with our own nothingness in His presence.

This example of "sickness of mind" which prevents prayer:

1) The hermit is very busy with something he has convinced himself to be "necessary work." He is building useless additions on to his cell, and going in for useless repair jobs.

2) He is being driven to this work by the tyranny of the devil, who urges him on with a red hot torch. In other words it is a burning and compulsive need for work that keeps him from his prayer; he is running away from himself and from God. Excessive work is his means of doing so.

3) So powerful is the influence of this "devil" that even natural fatigue cannot persuade him to sit down and rest. The importance of this is evident, because some who are infected with the same sickness interpret their symptoms as "zeal" and "generosity." But if they would listen to the voice of their conscience, and examine themselves with discretion, they would easily tell the difference between this and true zeal and generosity. For the latter is accompanied by peace and emptiness of self and is blessed by true obedience. Note: The cenobite can always extort permissions or commands to carry out the useless works to which he is attached. Yet in his heart of hearts he can tell that this is not true obedience.

4) This work of the devil is a mockery of God's image in man—"terrible trickery."

Cassian's conclusion: This worldly activism, this "ambition" which seeks to escape the inner solitude of the soul by the mirage of external accomplishments, is therefore not merely a matter of undertaking works foreign to the monastic state. What matters, says Cassian, is our care in restraining the need for undue work that is at hand, and tempts us by the appearance of necessity. In other words, generosity in the contemplative life and true zeal for prayer demands that we mortify the instinctive urge to get into activities which tempt us here and now and appear to be useful and necessary. We have to learn to confine our works within the limits of necessity and obedience, and beyond that to give our preference to prayer.

Cassian points out that the activities which are compatible with the monastic state as such, can become distracting and inordinate if they are allowed to take up too great a part of our life and push prayer into the background. In fact they can be just as distracting as greater and more ambitious projects belonging to the apostolate or to life in the world. Naturally we should also be detained from purely recreational activities. Each one needs work and a certain relaxation of mind, but to avoid disorder, we must follow obedience alone. Useless projects prevent true purity of heart. They prevent the monk from resting in God. They make the soul forget that God is its life and its joy, and they make it turn to other sources of satisfaction. This is in fact a spiritual death. We must be careful to keep our souls delicate and docile, responsive to the invitations of grace, and for this end we must not allow ourselves to be too much carried away with projects and activities which dull the spiritual sensibility of the soul. Work within reason refreshes the soul and helps prayer, but as soon as work becomes an outlet for self-love it ruins purity of heart. Neglect to mortify and control this desire for useless activity is the ruin of many potential contemplatives in our monasteries. But when our hearts are truly pure, then we live among the angels and no matter what we do, whether we work or pray, everything is transformed into pure prayer.

The Different Kinds of Prayer

Abbot Isaac begins his discussion of different kinds of prayer with true humility. Unlike the writers of familiar manuals and the readers of them for whom prayer becomes in theory such a clear and simple matter, Abbot Isaac reminds us of the fact that prayer is a mysterious and secret activity of the soul alone with God, and that it is rash to talk too glibly about it, because in fact "It is not possible to understand the various kinds of prayer without tremendous contrition of heart and purity of mind and the illumination of the Holy Ghost."

The first difficulty in explaining the "kinds of prayer" is that there is in reality an almost infinite variety. Prayer is always varying. It is a living reality and there are as many kinds of prayer as there are variations of spiritual states in all the different souls of men. The second half of chapter 8 is extremely wise, and Abbot Isaac reminds us that we pray differently under different circumstances, and in "classifying" prayer we must not forget these differences and these potential variations. In other words, we must not bind ourselves to pray always in the same way, or expect our prayer to fall always into the same pattern. We must not impose a rigid plan on our prayer life and try to make life conform to an abstract theory of our own, but we must on the contrary let our prayer be living, and let it grow out of our life in union with God. These cautions having been given, Abbot Isaac, following St. Paul, hesitantly suggests a possible division into four kinds of prayer, which may or may not cover the whole field of possibilities somehow. The four kinds of prayer (cf. 1 Tim. 2:1) are: Supplications, Prayers, Intercessions, Thanksgivings.

Supplication (*obsecratio*): The prayer of an earnest and contrite heart for the forgiveness of sin (783).

Prayers (*orationes*): Are especially those in which we offer, promise or vow something to God. Here the direction of the heart is to resolve something good and promise its accomplishment while praying for grace to carry it out, and desiring that God may be pleased with the offering, etc. "We pray when we renounce this world and pledge ourselves to die to all mundane acts and styles of living, and set ourselves to serve God with all our heart . . ." etc. The value of this prayer is proportionate to the sincerity of our intention to put into effect our good resolutions.

Intercessions (*postulationes*): Prayers offered for others in a time of fervor, whether for our own friends and relatives or for the peace of the world for the good of the whole Church. Here is where Cassian considers the monk's role as intercessor for others, "for all men, for Kings and for those in high positions." Here we have the monk's apostolate of prayer, the monk as the one who brings down grace upon the sinful world by his intercession. This is not just the official line!

Thanksgiving (*gratiarum actio*): These prayers well up from the heart which remembers the gifts of God, or contemplates His goodness and mercy in the present, or looks forward to the future fulfillment of His promises. Thanksgiving is not merely a cold and formal acknowledgement of these good things, but a deep and ardent expression of love in which we pray "through unspeakable ecstasies." This kind of prayer tends by its very nature to soar beyond words and clear concepts. It is marked by great purity (of faith, hope, and love) by immense joy, and by a kind of passivity ("our spirit is impelled"). They are prayers of *fire*.

The four kinds of prayer can be found alternately in one and the same person. Normally one of each type predominates in various degrees of the spiritual life. Supplication is more appropriate to the beginner who is not yet purged of his sins. Prayers are for the progressives who are advancing in virtue with confidence and faith. Intercessions are for the perfect who are able to pray for others with overflowing charity. Thanksgiving is for the purified soul (of the mystic?). These souls "with most pure minds are carried away with most burning hearts into that prayer of fire which the tongue of man can neither express nor comprehend." Note the originality of this doctrine: in any state or level man can sometimes offer pure and devout prayer—always a coalescence of all four. Important: out of all four comes the loftier state: contemplation of God alone; charity that burns like fire.

Cassian goes on to remark, however, that in the contemplative's "prayer of fire" all the kinds of prayer are likely to come together "in the form of an incomprehensible and most burning flame. . . ." In this prayer the Holy Spirit prays in us with "unutterable groanings" and the soul with great strength rises up to God filled with innumerable intentions and thoughts all in one moment, which, when left to itself, the soul could not conceive in a long stretch of time! At the same time, he will tell us later that this is not pure contemplation. The prayer of fire is related rather to *Theoria Physica* than to the highest contemplation. Also, sometimes in the very lowest form of prayer (compunction), the soul is raised to these same heights of fire by the vision of the divine mercy. To the higher degrees of prayer we must travel in a patient and orderly manner beginning at the bottom and working up. It is a great mistake to rush on ahead of grace in the spiritual life. We may be able to convince ourselves for a while that we are getting somewhere, but in the end we will only have to go back and cover more laboriously and with greater difficulty the ground we had passed over too rapidly.

Jesus made use of all these forms of prayer. Cassian turns to an analysis of the Lord's Prayer—a standard requisite for any early treatise on prayer. This is obvious because the *Pater* is the model of all Christian prayer. Let us never say it merely mechanically. The opening words, says Cassian, are an indication that it is God's will that we seek the *parrhesia* (familiar speech, the liberty of sons) lost by Adam—God is our Father, and He wills above all that we be united to Him in love and contemplation. Here Cassian sums up the constant tradition of the Fathers. Perfect contemplation is, he says, a state more sublime than anything included in the four kinds of prayer he has been discussing; this highest prayer has the following elements:

1) Contemplation and love of God alone. (It is the pure contemplation of the Trinity, not the *theoria* of God in creatures.)

2) The mind is taken out of itself, abandons itself, in pure love of God, and gives itself over to the most intimate and familiar union.

3) The soul then "converses" (not with words) with God with a very special kind of love.

The Lord's Prayer leads to perfect contemplation. Like St. Teresa of Avila [*The Way of Perfection*, ch. 25], Cassian affirms that if we pray the *Pater* really well it can lead us to higher degrees of prayer, notably to that prayer of fire already described. "This prayer (the *Pater*) leads those who practice it well to that higher state which we have described above, and brings them at last to that prayer of fire which is known and experienced by few and which is an inexpressibly high degree of prayer. . . ."

We must not be ungrateful of the slightest chance to grow in prayer, and must not despise the humble and ordinary opportunities offered us by God to do so. We must be ready for these special moments and touches of grace that awaken us from inertia. Here are some of them according to Cassian:

1) They can come with a verse of a psalm, which can provide an "occasion for the fire of prayer." The meanings of the psalms we sing are the primary and serious source of light in choral prayer. Hence St. Benedict's advice: "so sing the psalms that mind and voice may be in harmony" [*Rule*, c. 19]. The Psalms' principle is to make them so much our own that we experience them as poems we ourselves have written. This involves time, and patient rumination of texts, staying with one text until it is fully absorbed.

2) The fervor of our brethren in choir can excite us to greater compunction and attention in prayer—especially the distinctness and gravity with which they pronounce the psalms. (Cassian is thinking of the Egyptian office in which one monk chanted the psalm and the others listened.) With us the Gregorian melodies would have a comparable effect.

3) Spiritual conferences and exhortations given by the Fathers.

4) The death of someone dear to us can excite compunction and recollection and greatly aid our progress in prayer, reminding us of the last things and stirring us up to pray for or with the brother who has died and gone to his reward, sharing his victory in the Lord.

5) The remembrance of our own tepidity and negligence can excite in us salutary zeal for prayer.

In a word, Cassian declares that there are innumerable ways in which God stirs us up and awakens us out of our torpor, to keep us praying well.

Fervor is again equated with "compunction." The holy hermits, possessed with "unbearable joy," shout and cry out in their cells and can be heard at a great distance! At other times, the soul is overwhelmed by grace and reduced to total silence so that we cannot utter a word—profound interior silence. It is well to examine the language in which he describes this grace. He redoubles words for "silence," hiddenness, and inwardness. The "mens," that which is most inward in man, is "hidden in the secret depths of silence"—silences the sound of any word or the spirit may pour forth unutterable desires. Sometimes tears are the only outlet. He is talking of a simple form of contemplative prayer of beginners. Germanus readily admits he is familiar with this; however he thinks there is nothing more sublime. But he complains he cannot produce this at will. Is this possible?

In reply, Abbot Isaac describes different sources of "tears" with illustrations from the psalms. Some come from the memory of our sins. Some from the contemplation of our eternal reward, thirst for God and the desire of heaven. Some from fear of hell and of the Last Judgement. The sins of others can be a source of tears for us, also, [and] sorrow at the miseries of this present life. Finally, there are tears which are brought on by sheer force from "dry eyes." Cassian is willing to approve even these as being not without merit, but only in the case of the hardened sinner who has little or no knowledge of God. Those who have progressed a little in the spiritual life and have a taste for virtue are "by no means" to force themselves to weep as this would be very harmful, for it would prevent them from ever arriving at the grace of spontaneous tears.

Abbot Isaac [then] reverently brings in the name of Anthony the Great, the supreme model and doctor of prayer for the ancient Fathers. Anthony could pray whole nights "in the same ecstasy of spirit"—carried out of himself. Anthony's description of perfect prayer is qualified by Isaac as a "heavenly statement which is beyond all that is human"—(in other words, inspired by God). "He said, 'It is not perfect prayer in which a monk is conscious of himself or of what he is praying.'"[1] In the opinion of Isaac, this is the last word on prayer, to which nothing further may be added.

[1] This principle exists in other religious traditions, too—for example, in some of Martin Buber's most memorable tales of the early Hasidic masters.

Philoxenos of Mabbug

*M*ar[1] Philoxenos—the Monophysite bishop of Mabbug, is honored as a saint and doctor of the Church by the Jacobites, Copts, and Ethiopians. Mabbug (Hierapolis, today Mambidj) is located between Antioch and the Euphrates. He was born in Persia, studied at Edessa, and became bishop in 485 (elevated by the monophysite Patriarch of Antioch). He was exiled in 519 (because of monophysitism) and died in 523 at Gangres.

The importance of Philoxenos is that he combined the Syrian tradition of Aphraat and Ephrem with the Greco-Egyptian philosophical thought of Evagrius and Origen. His homilies, preached or read to monastic audiences, are free of monophysitism. His monophysitism depended on the fact that he took nature and person to be the same, though frequently saying Christ was both God and Man. He was closer to the Council of Chalcedon than to the monophysites condemned by the Council. He was so opposed to Nestorianism that he feared the term "two natures."

What are the three divisions of the spiritual life in Philoxenos? They correspond in general to the familiar beginners, progressives, perfect; or the three degrees of Pseudo-Denys: purgation,

---

[1] Merton has used the honorific "Mar" a few times already by this point in these lectures. "Mar" or "Mor" is a title of respect in Syriac which means, "my lord." "Mart" or "Mort" is the feminine.

illumination, union; or those of Origen—Evagrius: *praxis* (*ascesis*), *theoria physica, theologia*; or St. Bernard: slaves, faithful servants (hired servants, mercenaries), sons. Philoxenos uses the Biblical (Pauline) division, as does William of St. Thierry: *somatikoi* (animal man) fight against sins; *psychikoi* (rational man) fight against thoughts and demons; *pneumatikoi* (spiritual man) have reception of spiritual gifts. This division is specifically Syrian and not Greek.

For Philoxenos, the first degree [of the spiritual life] equals ascesis in the cenobitic life (after the passage over the Red Sea, entering the monastery). The second degree equals passage to the solitary life in the cell (crossing the Jordan, entering the Promised Land and fighting the "seven nations"). The third degree equals attaining the height of contemplation in solitude.

Foundations of the Spiritual Life (Homily 1)

The basic idea is order in the spiritual life. Discipline involves starting at the beginning and going on from there. Prelude: the importance of starting, of recognizing the need to work, and not merely of being a "hearer of the word" who does nothing. He who simply reads the word without responding in his actions is like a dead man over whom a thousand trumpets are blown. He does not move. So failure to respond to the word of God in action is a sign that the will is dead. In apprenticeship and education, the master begins by having the pupil carry out the smallest tasks. Wrestlers and fighters are first taught the basic position which sets them "on guard," then the first hold; after that they wrestle. In a palace, the new courtiers are taught by the old ones how to walk, how to conduct themselves and speak before the king.

The basis of the spiritual life is the struggle against the passions. The novice must learn how the passions of the body work, what temptations to expect, how to confront them, and then he will later learn the more difficult combat against the passions of the soul (cf. Cassian). This means also learning what passions arise as a result of our good works. Certain passions are born of fasting, others of psalmody, vigils, etc.

We must know what passion is born in the soul from fasting of the body, from continency, from psalmody in choir, from prayer in silence, from renunciation of property, austerity of clothing—what passion awakens in us when our rule is better than that of our brother, what passions come to us from the science of thought, what passion we fall into when we have overcome the love of the stomach for food, what other awakens against us when we have finally triumphed in the war against fornication; what passion is born in us from obedience to bishops, and what from obedience towards all; and what are the thoughts that are in us when we rebel against obedience; and by what teaching thoughts of indocility to the masters are overcome; by what thought we escape from the presumption of our own knowledge; etc.

This will then be a study of great psychological subtlety. He will also play one passion against the other. For the beginner it is important to: concentrate on special commandments important for them; obey their masters without paying attention to the faults of these latter; learn how to profit from the good works they do; how to conduct themselves in the cells of their brethren; the measure of fasting—fasting of body, fasting of soul, fasting of spirit; how to overcome antipathies to other monks; how to fight distractions in the time of silence and how to keep alive in the soul the passion for God and the desire for pure prayer; how to recognize by experience the harm done by unnecessary human contacts, conversations, etc. Only if he knows these things can the beginner advance with confidence in the way of his vocation.

Hence the first rule of all for the beginner is to recognize that he is a disciple, that he does not know these things, and that he must learn.

Beginners must be prepared to receive the knowledge of these things from masters, just as the apprentice receives his training from his master. Further reasons: this knowledge is a new kind, a supernatural knowledge. Hence it has to be received through someone appointed by God. And if one is attached to his own natural knowledge, he cannot receive the supernatural knowledge. He becomes detached from his own knowledge and judgement by tears of repentance and humility. "It is only then that he will approach the banquet hall of the divine mysteries clad in the spiritual garments that are required if he is to enter."

[The] duty of the Master: he must "consider himself as a tutor to whom are entrusted the children of a heavenly king, having a King for Father, a king for brother, a queen for mother. And just as those who educate the children of a worldly king apply themselves with infinite care to form them and strive through the children to please the parents . . . so the master must be greatly attentive to his disciples and to their care and their progress." We are all physicians entrusted with the health of one another. The remedy for every illness is found in the word of God. In the word of God we seek the proper remedy, the contrary to the sickness: i.e., faith, against doubt, etc. Here follows what is practically a list of instruments of good works. The résumé of all these works is that death of the physical desire is necessary before spiritual desire is born in the soul. The principle is that wherever there is a sickness there is a natural remedy near at hand. Our remedies are within reach, but we have to know our sicknesses and desire the remedies.

What Is Simplicity? (Homily 4)

1) True simplicity is acquired only in the desert.

2) Only simplicity can please God.

Man is made simple by nature. He comes simple from the hand of God. Society endows him with craftiness and duplicity. If a man were to remain in the desert, untouched by social influences, he would remain simple; and the characteristic of simplicity is that it attributes nothing to itself but sees all as coming from God. Even in monasteries perfect simplicity is not always found (*Hom.* 5). Ruse and craftiness exist in an atmosphere of "dealing, of buying and selling, of trading," the adjustment of mutual advantage. Hence even in the monastery words may be spoken with the intention to mislead or to deceive. With this there may be a tendency to mock true simplicity. But the simple monk should not be ashamed of his childlikeness and his guilelessness. For the simple are essential to the Kingdom of God.

Unity [is found in] single-mindedness. "It hears the word of God without judging it and receives it without questioning it." Abraham heard the word of God, held it at once as completely true, and obeyed without afterthought. "Abraham ran toward the word of God as a child to his Father, and all things became contemptible in his eyes as soon as he had heard God's word."

> The Apostles did not require a long instruction: they needed only to hear the word of faith. Since their faith was alive, as soon as it received the living voice it obeyed the voice of life; they ran at once after Christ and made no delay to follow Him; by this it was evident that they were disciples even before they were called.

Simple faith does not require arguments, but as the healthy eye responds directly to light, so it responds directly to the living word of God (cf. St. Anselm, *Proslogion*). This implies a mind free from the tyranny of social prejudice and bad habits of thought acquired through conformism in the world. "The Apostles obeyed like living men and went forth unburdened because nothing in the world impeded them with its weight. Nothing can bind and impede the soul that is aware of God: it is open and ready, so that the light of the divine voice, whenever it appears, finds the soul ready and receptive."

Readiness [is important]: Zacchaeus "hoped to see Jesus and become his disciple even before he was called." He had already believed the report of others. This is simplicity (cf. Homily of St. Gregory the Great on Zacchaeus.) The temptation of Adam:

the simplicity of obedience is divided into "two wills" by temptation—this duplicity puts Adam in a position where he presumes to judge the divine command. But in this case he did not show real autonomy; he obeyed the deceit of the enemy, not the simplicity of the divine will. This is an erroneous concept of liberty—the presumption that liberty consists in judging reality and deciding not to conform to it! The Apostles were deliberately chosen for their simplicity, to confound the wise of the world.

> Where is the one who is wise? Where is the scribe? Where is the debater of this age? Has not God made foolish the wisdom of the world? (1 Cor. 1:20)

Adam and Eve before the Fall knew nothing of "worldly affairs"—which were simply irrelevant to their state. God was always with them, taking them wherever they went. He showed them everything from near at hand like a man. And they received no thought about Him in their Spirit. They never asked: Where does He live who shows us these things? How long has He existed? And if He created all else, was He also created? And we, why has He created us? Why has He placed us in this Paradise? Why has He given us this Law? All these things were far from their minds, because simplicity does not think such things, but is completely absorbed in listening to what it hears, and all its thought is mingled with the word of him who speaks, as is the little child absorbed in the one who speaks to him. So, then, God put simplicity into the first leaders of our race, and it was to simplicity that he gave the first commandment.

Later, Philoxenos adds, in another connection: "God has chosen ignorant ones who do not imagine, when they have learned His word, that it is *their* word, but they know Him who has spoken and give thanks to Him."

At our birth, simplicity is at work in us before craftiness. When children grow in the world they learn deceit by acting and growing. [Philoxenos teaches:] If someone were to take a year-old child and bring him up in the desert where there is no occupation of men and no use of the things of this world, where he will see absolutely nothing of the activity of men, the child can maintain himself in all the simplicity of nature even when he has attained to the age of man, and he can quite easily perceive divine visions and spiritual thoughts and can promptly become a receptacle that will accept the divine wisdom. Note: compare here the idea of man's natural simplicity in Chinese thought (Mencius).[2]

"If deceit and wickedness are acquired by education in the world, it is certain that simplicity and innocence are acquired by training and occupation in silence, and that the more one dwells in silence, the simpler one becomes (Philoxenos)." Texts from the Psalms on simplicity are quoted and commented on. He does not even hesitate to call Jacob an example of simplicity—because he obeyed his mother in tricking Isaac! (Which in fact is not far from the mind of the Yahwist; Jacob did what he was told and the Lord took care of everything for him.) "Thou therefore, O disciple, remain in the purity of thy spirit. It is for the Lord to know how He will guide thy life and He will deal with thee as is best for thee," [says Philoxenos in the homily]. Note the special aspect of "purity of heart." In all things and in all trials the essential thing is to remain with one's gaze towards God in trust and simplicity, not concerned with plans of our own.

Hope is shown as the stabilizing power of simplicity:

> Remain simple with regard to all that you hear, and let
> those who talk about you not change you and not make

---

[2] "See Merton's translation of the 'Ox Mountain Parable' of Meng Tzu (Mencius) at the end of his essay 'Classic Chinese Thought,' in Thomas Merton, *Mystics and Zen Masters* (New York: Farrar, Straus and Giroux, 1967), 65–68. See also his comments on the text in *Conjectures of a Guilty Bystander* (Garden City, NY: Doubleday, 1966), 123, where he concludes, 'Without the night spirit, the dawn breath, silence, passivity, rest, man's nature cannot be itself. In its barrenness it is no longer *natura*: nothing grows from it, nothing is born of it any more.'" –Patrick O'Connell

you become as they are. For the adversary brings all this about in order to turn your spirit away from its meekness, to disturb and trouble your purity of heart, to make your simplicity deceitful, so that you will become like those who fight against you, that you may be filled with anger as they are and become a vessel of wrath like unto them, putting on the garment of iniquity.

"Simplicity is the vessel which receives the revelations of God." Simplicity in Philoxenos has the same function as Purity of Heart in Cassian.

Letter to a Converted Jew

This is a letter of encouragement and advice to a converted Jew who is seeking union with God in the monastic life. Its theme of the full development of the New Man in silence and solitude is characteristic of Philoxenos. Christ leads the Christian into solitude to defend him and lead him to full maturity and to the experience of God and spiritual joy.

Introduction: "You have begun well; you are following the way of knowledge and thus we may hope you will attain to wisdom."

The two ways: asceticism and knowledge. Corporal asceticism consists in the works that are necessary for true knowledge, which is not acquired from words or books. "Words beget nothing but words and if one sets out to find Christ by words, one finds only words before him." "But if one seeks knowledge by labors and austerities then this knowledge in person appears before him and lets herself be touched by him and leads him to ascend her highest steps."

Steps:

a) a detachment from pleasure to attain to virtue;

b) detachment from the world to attain to knowledge. Silence is the way to this. Note the importance of silence as the way to knowledge. It is silence that marks the transition from active asceticism to inner detachment and spiritual knowledge. "If you love silence then I know that you have experienced Christ Himself. If one does not understand the word of the wise man, one does not love to live with him, and if one has not first experienced the power of Christ, one does not love the silence that brings us close to Him."

Two reasons for choosing silence:

a) One may live with a Master because one experiences the power of his word and one may choose silence because one has purity of heart and experiences God.

b) Or one can follow a Master because of his reputation, and one can love silence because one has been told it is good.

"Material silence introduces us into spiritual silence and spiritual silence raises man to life in God; but if man ceases to live in silence he will have no converse with God. Hence, as long as the mind has not silenced all the trepidations and agitation of the world it will not even begin to stammer a little conversation with God."

Philoxenos emphasizes the importance of interior silence—calming down before trying seriously to pray. The new man is a "man of silence"—there is a relationship of silence and joy. But again there are two levels: by grace (of the Sacrament) one puts on the new man but does not experience this silence; by the practice of joy one experiences the silence of the Spirit. This means getting rid of all the old man by renunciation, and putting on all the new man, made in the likeness of God. If one does not completely renew himself in Christ, the old man becomes merely "the tomb in which the new man is buried." (Conflicts of monastic life are due to this!)

Asceticism is perfected in silence—purity of body rejects desires but does not see God—but purity of heart rejects inmost thoughts of flesh and does see God. One should desire to have

Christ always by one's side. He is the perfect model. The spiritual man must see himself with Christ on one side and Satan on the other, and he must rely always on the power of Christ.

Letter to a Novice

There is hope for progress when the novice has:

a) "taken root in the earth of doctrine."

b) been "consoled by the hope that gives strength." This is hope in God, not in one's own powers; it is based on a remembrance of the life one led in the world when abandoned to his own ideas, and gratitude for the grace that called one out of the world, an awareness that this grace puts us in debt and we must pay our debt to Christ, by fidelity to the knowledge He has given us of his love.

The novice must put into his monastic life all the zeal and energy with which he formerly followed the things of the world. Perseverance is based on a "taste" for the things of God: "Receive the taste for Christ who has called you; this sense of taste is in the understanding; taste the chalice in secret; each thing is tasted in its proper place, and through those things which are related to it. The bodily senses taste the desires of the world, while the understanding of the soul tastes the sweetness of Christ." Remembering Lot's wife, the novice must not look back.

Other aids include:

a) constant thought of the presence of God;

b) not associating with dissolute monks;

c) strict discipline, austerity;

d) readiness to carry out humiliating tasks in the interests of the monastery, motivated by the humility with which Christ rendered services to his disciples;

e) prayer: awareness of the mysteries of Christ, especially the crucifixion;

f) psalmody: "If you put your heart in the psalm you will learn, and if you enclose your mind in the verses of your office you will fill up what is wanting in the Passion";

g) obedience even to one's juniors, when occasion offers;

h) silence: not seeking to hear news;

i) never mocking anyone;

j) not undertaking great things without being proficient in little things; not multiplying ascetic practices beyond one's strength;

k) stability: "Do not move from one monastery to another even if you think you are prevented from doing works of mortification where you are. Rather apply yourself to confronting the difficulties of the place where you are";

l) reading.

Courage and humility are developed in overcoming our actual faults. "There is nothing greater in this world for us than to show, on the occasion of some fault, great or small, heroic strength of soul, and not allow ourselves to be downcast." (Note the use of faults to face the truth. Control of thoughts is crucial.)

Note the supreme importance of humility and obedience for beginners. Without humility and obedience the ascetic life has no foundations. See *Letter on Monastic Life* [as well]: "The first virtue which must be possessed by those who receive the habit must be humility, from which is born obedience, which is a fruit of the spirit . . . and from which all good actions are born." Then he quotes: "He humbled himself . . . obedient unto death" (Phil. 2:8). As the disobedience of Adam brought into the world all evils, "so true obedience prepares, for him who possesses it, all the consolations and delights of the Spirit."

The qualities of obedience are then described:

> It does not consist in a man doing what he pleases . . . but in cutting away all his own will and doing the will of him

to whom he has surrendered himself once for all, even if this is displeasing by reason of the carnal desires still in himself. If you do what you like, and do not do what is hard to you, you prove that you are not obedient and that you serve your own will.

Joshua and Caleb are given as models of obedience (Numbers 13), while all the others, disobedient, perished in the desert. So the cenobite who wishes to go and live in a cell (symbolized by the "promised land") must first prove himself perfectly obedient in community.

On the other hand, stubborn disobedience is the root of all vices. This is described in relation to Exodus 32. Fixing one's eyes on the "serpent" of the obedient Christ (Numbers 14) saves one from the serpent of calumny and unjust reproach, so often met in the desert. So, too, for all other trials: "By His crucifixion Jesus is nearer to you than the brazen serpent was to the Jews for He dwells in your heart, and in the secret recesses of your soul there shines the radiance of His glorious visage."

Vocation to the Desert (Homily 9)

Christ going out into the desert is the model of monastic renunciation. The monk, like Christ, goes into the desert to engage in combat with the spiritual enemy. He must not take anything of the world with him. He leaves the world in the "Jordan" or the "Red Sea" on his way into the desert. The Holy Spirit accompanies those who go out into the desert, but only if they rely on no other source of strength. "The disciples who abandon the company of the world are at once aided by the Spirit, and when they have despised human help they win celestial assistance; as soon as they reject bodily strength, spiritual strength is given to them at once." (Here the world is considered as an end in itself, a closed system in which individual survival is cared for.)

Jesus before and after baptism: Before baptism Jesus is subject to the Law. After it, He has no law but the Spirit and the will of His Father. "Man is born from one world into another when he passes from the rule of the world to the rule of Christ, and from being the master of possessions to the renunciation that God asks of him. When a man is in the world he is subject to a rule that demands that he do all those things of the world; when he is gone out after Jesus it is demanded of him that he fulfill the spiritual law, according to the order of the place into which he is come." This last phrase refers not to a written or traditional set of rules, but to the mode of life dictated by the very nature of the desert. Really going out of the world means giving away all one's goods to the poor and "coming forth naked as one came forth from the womb."

He insists that going out into the desert is really a new birth. This throws much light on the traditional doctrine of religious profession as a second baptism.[3] It is in so far as it is a death and a resurrection to a new life. A mere change of worldly habits into other worldly habits will not suffice. (Note the ambiguity of Philoxenos' concept: Christian life "in the world" for him is insufficient. Is this the Biblical concept?) The new life entails "renouncing one's own thoughts, errors and ignorance." What is this ignorance?

The child in the womb of the world: Though baptized and "saved" the Christian in the world lives only in the same way that a child in the womb lives. He is alive, but he cannot make use of his senses. Hence he is blind and helpless, spiritually:

> The man who is shut up in the rule of the world like a child in the womb, has his discernment buried in the obscurity of cares . . . and human preoccupations; he cannot taste the riches of the rule of Christ and he does not see spiritual things . . .
>
> The spiritual foetus, having accomplished all the justice of the law in the world, as though in the womb, goes forth from the world as by a new birth . . . he begins a new

---

[3] Was mentioned in the context of St. Jerome in Lecture 8.

> growth and becomes perfect . . . not in the body of justice
> which is in the world but in the spiritual person who will
> reach the fullness of Christ.

Note the well-developed concept of spiritual maturity here. Good works in the world by no means constitute perfection. They are only the life and growth of the foetus in the womb of ignorance. "The foetus cannot become a man in the womb and man cannot become perfect in the world. No matter how the foetus in the womb develops, he cannot develop beyond the limits of the womb that encloses him: the justice of the Christian is confined to the limits of the womb of the world in which he is enclosed."

The trauma of spiritual birth: We are born to spiritual life in the world by the sacrament and by faith—that is to say by "hearing" only, by being told of the mystery of Christ and of our participation in Christ. But now we must actually experience in our lives the sufferings and death of Christ. "Now the time has come to will to leave the old man and to experience the fact that we leave him, by our labors and our weariness, and not just by the hearing of faith, by experience, by sufferings and tears, by love for God and pure prayers, by continual petitions, by wonder and contemplation of God's majesty, and by the rapid progress of the hidden man toward the Lord." The true maturity of the Christian is in that knowledge of God that is granted only in the desert. The justification of the Christian by faith and baptism is real but it is not a matter of experience, only of hearsay. He must experience the new life that comes from liberation from the passions and desires. Error and ignorance are closely associated with desire. They are born in the "service of desire" and "when the heart is hardened in delights." In order to live serving one's desires one must maintain a false concept of the meaning of life, centered on the self.

What balance is to be maintained? Man is made up of body and soul. But according to Philoxenos, it would be an error to say that we must therefore treat the body and the soul on an equal basis. Hence the "measure" or "golden mean" of natural virtue is not enough. One must first bring the body into complete submission to the soul, and this means giving it less than it might reasonably require. He will treat this in a later Homily, "Against Gluttony." To live even reasonably in the world, while amassing riches (even though one does so without injustice) is a life of weariness, frustration (cf. Ecclesiastes):

> What fatigue is more painful than to be wearied when one
> seeks to rest? The way of human riches is a way without
> end in the world. The further one advances, the further
> one must go. It has no end but death. If you accumulate
> riches in order to rest, even your rest becomes weariness,
> and if even the delights of the world are heavy labors and
> burdens, what shall we call its labor? . . . Those who seek
> the good things of the world bear heavy burdens. They
> wear themselves out seeking loss.

But "the true rich man is not he who has many things but he who has need of nothing . . ." "The more the rich man enriches himself the more he is poor. . . . The rich man is charmed by the love of what does not exist." This theme of the weariness of the good things of life, seen to be burdensome, is familiar (cf. Gregory of Nyssa, *Commentary on Ecclesiastes*). Thus, though a man may be rich and still be a "just man," he cannot attain to the perfection and the knowledge of God that are possible only in renunciation.

The Jordan: "Christ at the Jordan ended the road of the law and began the road of perfection which he showed by His passion to those who love Him. . . . The Jordan was for Him the passage from one world to the other, from the world of the body to the world of the Spirit." After the Jordan:

a) Jesus fulfills the will of no one but the Father;

b) He takes with Him nothing of the world, no law of the world, no human rule or measure. "He went out alone with

no one to help Him and without company, without friends
to care for Him, without precious things, without riches,
without possessions, without clothes, without ornaments;
nothing of the world went forth with him but only Himself
in the company of the Holy Spirit. Model thyself thus on
the going out of thy master; go out also having with thee
nothing of the world and the Holy Spirit will go with thee."

c) One of the chief reasons for going forth without burdens
is that the world pursues us into the desert and seeks to
win us back. If we have anything in us belonging to the
world, the world has a claim on us. "Cast off the burdens
of the world in order to fight the world." What this means
especially is not only the physical renunciation implicit in
our going forth, but especially the renunciation of worldly
thoughts and desires, the renunciation of the fundamental error which is in the service of desires, and which centers on care of the self and its protection. Our cares will
be left in the "Red Sea" like the Egyptians if we are generous and knowing in our renunciation. "Wash thyself in the
waters of knowledge rather than in the Jordan and having
washed, go forth in the Rule of the Spirit." There are then
two baptisms: the second leads into the desert.

Conditions of perseverance in the desert: This is a life of pure
praise, the life of the Kingdom of God, not of man. Here is nothing but tranquillity and spiritual repose, all the inhabitants sing
out the Trisagion in praise of the Holy Essence. All you know is
that you have joy, but you know not how to explain whence that
joy comes. Instead of conversation with men you have conversation with Jesus Christ, and you sustain your labors without weariness because the awareness of Christ does not allow you to
feel them and the ravishment of your mind in God makes you
unable to feel bodily things. In your spiritual understanding are
deposited the spiritual signs of divine knowledge, not in symbol

but in truth because knowledge comes to meet knowledge without intermediary. "Here is no altar of gold on which incense is offered but the altar of the Spirit where all good and reasonable thoughts go up."

Important: all the signs, symbols, rites etc. that were used collectively by the People of God are here realized in the spiritual person. The worship of the spiritual person in solitude is then the fulfillment of all these signs in collective worship. The sacrifice offered to God here is more pleasing than that of outward liturgy: "Here is the living table which is Christ Himself. . . . Here the high priest Himself, Christ, consecrates before His Father living and reasonable substances." The condition of remaining in this kingdom is then "to work legitimately in this place according to the justice of the place," that is to say in the spirit, in contemplation, and not according to the rule of the world, in outward works and signs. One must get rid both of "bodily rules" and of "dead thoughts." One must live by the spiritual rule, *conversatio nostra in coelis* ("our citizenship is in heaven").

One must not only fulfill the external actions of the desert life (solitude, silence, etc.), but one must think the thoughts of the spiritual world in which one now dwells. This calls for unequivocal renunciation of the world in all thoughts. One must not remain linked to the world even by the smallest thoughts and desires (here he uses the famous image of the bird held by a thread). Note—like St. John of the Cross [in *Ascent of Mount Carmel*], Philoxenos also mistrusts visions and other extraordinary psychological experiences. "St. Paul says that all that the tongue can represent of contemplation in the region of bodily beings is nothing but a phantom of the thoughts of the mind and not an effect of grace. Consequently you must remember this and be on your guard against the phantasies of deep thoughts [unconscious images]" (from the *Letter to Patricius*). The inordinate desire of contemplative experiences is therefore reproved.

The Kingdom of Heaven: true science comes when one is no longer "bound" by the ignorance which imagines that the things of the world are definitively real. This means freedom from cares and anxieties about the things of the world. The knowledge that comes to one who is free from care is twofold:

1) He perceives "the spiritual rule" as a beginner;

2) As a progressive and perfect man he sees and dwells in the Kingdom of God.

The Kingdom of Heaven (enjoyed even on earth by the wise) is freedom from all care, because free of illusion. Philoxenos says: "The Kingdom of Heaven is a soul without passions, having knowledge of that which is." The passions bring care because they bring fear of loss—hence also mistrust, anxiety. When one has forsaken care about worldly things and about one's own life on earth, then there is no room for anxiety. All is joy and hope. This joy is a foretaste of the joy of heaven itself. The Kingdom of Heaven on earth then consists in a beginning of the future life by the foretaste which is given us in: perfect trust; Eucharistic union with Christ, foreshadowing perfect union with His Person in Heaven; union with the Holy Spirit in faith, presaging the perfectly known union with Him in Heaven.

Hence it becomes important to study the "rule of perfection" which is the way to the "Kingdom of Heaven." He mentions living examples of the rule of perfection: John the Baptist is the model of solitaries. He never sinned. He possessed the Holy Spirit from his mother's womb. "He received the Spirit even in the womb and grew up out of the world so that by these means he might possess the purity of the first man before he transgressed the commandment, and by this purity of soul he received the knowledge of the divine mysteries." The rule of perfection is then the solitary life, in freedom, and far from men, avoiding all human conversation. This is the complete renunciation demanded by Christ in Luke 14:26 and Luke 9:60. Commenting on this latter passage ("Let the dead bury the dead"), Philoxenos paraphrases it:

> It is not necessary for you to observe the law because I have observed it and have loosed it. It is not necessary to serve your natural parents because I have served them for all. Hence the yoke of the law of nature is lifted off you and you are left free to yourself in such manner that the world cannot oblige you to serve it, since it is dead to you and you are dead to it. One does not serve corpses. . . . Let the corpses bury each other.

On not looking back (Luke 9:61), he has Christ say: "I have come to divide a man against his father. . . . I brought the sword and you want to go and salute your relatives? . . . You run to sew up with your foolishness the rent that I have torn in the world. . . . I have torn this mantle of agreement because it was entirely woven in errors, and in its place I have woven the mantle of heavenly salvation." Hence the need of perfect interior detachment in thought, to accord with the exterior signs of detachment, the monastic habit, tonsure, etc.

On Fornication (Homily 12)

Why does the natural desire (of marriage) persist in the ascetic? For his advantage, to teach him the power of spiritual love. The disciple needs to experience the force and heat of the desire of the Spirit by experiencing the heat of natural desire.

When the fire of lawlessness is kindled in their members, they can also experience the burning fire that Jesus has placed in them. Then, instead of unnatural pleasure they experience the joys of our true nature. Instead of the movements [of lust] which end as soon as they have begun, the disciple tastes the joy of living movement which begins with a desire to see the beauty of Christ and remains without end in the soul purified to be its worthy habitation.

Hence, the thing to do is to make good use of temptation in order to grow spiritually by it, and not be ruined by it. At the same time, one who has experienced the joys and light of the spirit has greater cause for sorrow and shame if he allows himself to compromise with impure thoughts. But this can teach them the need for vigilance in thoughts, and make them realize that the avoidance of lustful actions is not enough. If one finds himself thinking of bodily beauty, he must realize this is because he does not see the beauty of God. "It is for lack of beauty that you desire beauty." Desire would not have real force against us unless we allowed it to grow strong and blind us (at least unconsciously). We must "teach the soul to live solitary in the house of the body," that is to say, to become aware of itself as not identified completely with the body and its desires.

> Though dwelling in the body the pure soul does not participate in its passions. It does not unite the mystery of its love with that which does not deserve love, but living apart and solitary, in admiration at the greatness of God's glory, it dwells in a house of silence.

> A solitary mind is that which, living in the body, is a stranger and remote from all its desires and pleasures, and is with itself.

When the soul is "solitary" in the body it can summon to itself all the natural energies and use them against the passions (or withdraw their use from the passions, rather).

The allies of desire: The body alone has not strength to overcome the soul. But it entices to itself the energies of the soul by pleasures of eating and drinking; all pleasure and recreation— "play"; fine clothes; conversation turning upon pleasures, desires, lusts; contemplating faces, bodies; daydreams; memories. To fight desire, "take away fuel and the flames will go out." He advises "fury" against even small inclinations to the above. (Note: exaggerated effort and agitation do more harm than good. Peaceful, positive, turning away is more effective.) He admits anger is an evil, but use passion to fight passion in the beginning, he says. He points out the special danger of supposedly "spiritual friendships."

Importance of awareness of God's presence: In order to yield to sinful desires, the soul seeks darkness and oblivion of God. If one is aware of God, he cannot surrender to sin. Hence, keep the light of awareness burning, and you will not yield to temptation.

Only the light of God's presence can restrain the soul from sins of the flesh; thus it must always preserve this light in itself, that it may continually shine there. The soul must not let the memory of God depart, but must be held by the pleasure of converse with Him. As long as the soul converses with Him it will not abase itself to converse with its desire. As long as the light of God shines in the soul, the darkness does not enter, as into its own house, into this place of light. As long as the desire of the soul is mingled with the desire of the Holy Spirit, it does not mingle its thoughts with the desire of the flesh.

However, it is clear that the body may independently have desires which the soul does not accept. Union of the soul with God in charity does not exclude all bodily feelings. On the contrary, the combat of the monk consists in keeping the soul detached, untouched, even though desires may rage. Philoxenos recommends that we try to draw spiritual profit from inevitable desires, studying them objectively, without panic, trying to learn the causes. According to Philoxenos, the monk even permits the heat of desire to grow, in order to observe how it works. But this, we may add, is dangerous. For instance he suggests that the ascetic ought to be able to arouse impure desires and quiet them again by an act of will. Philoxenos supposes that the intelligence will remain cool, objective and detached and not be blinded by desire itself. But the danger is that while the mind imagines itself cool and detached, it has perhaps already been blinded and deceived:

> If you have confidence in the power of the mind do not be alarmed by the movement of desire in your members; it is the occasion of much good for you, if you have knowledge and can draw profit from this trial instead of loss.

He admits this will not work as long as "the thought is seized by the sweetness of the desire." It must be entirely untouched. The condition of "drawing profit" is that one should struggle manfully to make one's desire of God greater and more fervent than is the ardor of lust in the body.

Later, Philoxenos admits that if the mind is not sure of remaining free from desire, it should take flight from the combat and not try to gain knowledge by calmly observing the rise of passion. The practice requires a cool, objective power to observe without being affected by what one sees. This is not to be recommended as a tactic, especially for beginners. One can easily be misled by false confidence, and if it works one may still be confirmed in pride. Philoxenos recognizes this himself. A victory based on vainglory is of no value. Victory must come from God. The real remedy is trust in grace, not in "the power of the mind." However, there is no harm in remaining calm and objective and not giving in to useless fears. Fasting remains supremely important, because an abundance of food is like oil on the flames (of lust).

Conclusions:

1) To understand this treatment of fornication in which the ascetic combats it not only by flight but by direct attack, the usual outlook of Philoxenos must be remembered. "All teaching that comes from outside us accumulates in us through the medium of words. But the doctrine that we acquire by overcoming passion establishes wisdom in us by the experience of the fact itself. Such knowledge is worthy of confidence and is truly certain. And when the soul finds this wisdom, this is more pleasing to it than that which comes from outside because it is of our own household,

and by it the soul rests in itself, its joy coming from within itself and not from the outside." "Therefore observe [your passions] with the discernment of knowledge, understand and distinguish between your person and your passion, so that you may make haste to seek the purity of your person."

2) Overcoming passion by passion is only a beginning. It is not real victory but only "containment" of passion. Here the desire of self-knowledge is regarded merely as a passion and its victories are not secure. The other passion may come back and win. True victory comes from the love of the Holy Spirit overcoming the lust of the body. This is the "divine triumph," the only true victory. The great thing is then not to gain knowledge by experiment with passion but to surrender completely to the Holy Spirit, to be led by Him, so that all our actions are spiritualized.

Group Discussion Topics, Questions, and Additional Readings

Lecture 1

In her book, *The New Asceticism*, British theologian Sarah Coakley recently said: "[We are] titillated intellectually by antique ascetic rigour, but for the most part quite unthinkingly accommodated to post-modern self-indulgence. Asceticism [has] become voyeuristic, something to study but not actually *do*" (18). Does this strike you as accurate of many today who read a book such as this? How might this contrast with Merton's original audience of young men studying to become Trappist monks?

Note the "mystique of martyrdom" and the quotes from Tertullian and St. Cyprian praising the actions of a martyr. These are sobering, particularly in a time when it is often presumed that these ideas are only owned by fundamentalists of other religious traditions.

Lecture 2

Among the many "Aberrations" in this Lecture is Montanism; Merton only briefly mentions one of the aspects of that error: ecstasy. Montanus, for whom Montanism is named, was known for ecstatic prophecy and trance. His was the essence of the mystic's myth that there are secrets to be known and that one must be initiated by particular experiences in order to come to know those mysteries. A century ago, the Quaker scholar, Rufus Jones, explained it this way in his book, *Studies in Mystical Tradition* (1909):

Montanism did not introduce new doctrines; it was not a
new conception of God, nor of the world, nor of salvation.
It was rather an attempt to realise in the Church the
promise of Christ that the Paraclete should come to lead
men into all truth and to enable them to do *greater things*
than He did. (39)

Lecture 3

In his *Stromata*, Clement of Alexandria begins the Christian
tradition of understanding prayer as much more than simply
talking with God. This is part of what's essential in the desert
tradition—and perhaps a corrective needed for Christians today,
for whom prayer is learned most often as conversation not unlike what takes places between friends.

> Prayer is . . . converse with God. Though whispering . . .
> and not opening the lips, we speak in silence, yet we cry
> inwardly. For God hears continually all the inward con-
> verse. So also we raise the head and lift the hands to heaven
> and set the feet in motion . . . following the eagerness of
> the spirit directed towards the intellectual essence; and
> endeavoring to abstract the body from the earth along with
> the discourse, raising the soul aloft, winged with longing
> for better things, we compel it to advance to the region of
> holiness, magnanimously despising the chain of the flesh.

[This is the English translation of *Stromateis*, from book seven,
available at http://newadvent.org/fathers/02107.htm.]

This is prayer of the heart, with an intensity of intention and
devotion that does not resemble, for instance, how the Lord's
Prayer is often taught to Christians, as simple conversation with
one's Abba. Clement's way of prayer (like that of Evagrius, later)
is about salvation: made possible through redemption in Christ,
seeking relationship to God and holiness and salvation through
(not at all simple) conversation.

1) How do you understand prayer?

2) Do Clement's words, and the desert tradition, add something important to your practice of prayer?

Lecture 4

Recently in *Cistercian Studies Quarterly*, Tim Vivian wrote about St. Anthony and the document we know as the "Sayings" of the Desert Fathers. He asks the simple question, "Why read this stuff?" Then, Vivian answers the question. In his translation, the third saying begins: "Someone asked Abba Antony, saying, 'What sort of practices do I need to maintain in order to please God?'" Vivian summarizes the practical answers that come throughout the Sayings, attaching the Saying number for each. These include:

- Keep God right before your eyes, with you always. (3, 28)
- Hold on to the testimony of the Scriptures. (3)
- Stay put. (3, 31)
- Own up to your own errors. (4)
- Expect temptation to your last breath. (4)
- Don't be self-righteous. (6)
- Let go of the past. (6)

There are twenty-two more on Vivian's list. Make your own list.

[Tim Vivian, "Each Breath Both Prayer and Practice: The Sayings of Antony the Great in the Alphabetical Apophthegmata Patrum, A New Translation and Commentary," *Cistercian Studies Quarterly*, Vol. 53.3, 2018.]

Lecture 5

The second paragraph is telling of where Merton was at, personally, when these lectures were first delivered:

> With Pachomius, we find organized community life. And here begins an old debate: between cenobites and hermits. It was to last a long time, and the thread of argument runs all through the Desert Fathers' literature. Some are for the free, unorganized life of the hermit living alone with God. Others are for the safer, more consistent, organized life of communities. The argument sometimes gets quite heated, and in the end the cenobites, for all practical purposes, won out. The eremitical ideal remains still the highest ideal of monasticism . . .

How does the "debate" between community life and hermit life in monasticism relate to the "debate" between parish life and individual spirituality for the average Christian? For you?

Lecture 6

Renouncing the world, leaving the world, forsaking the world—are constant themes throughout these Lectures. Merton famously changed his view of the monk as one who "leaves" the world when he realized one day at the corner of 4th and Walnut, in downtown Louisville, a connection to everyone around him, that everyone was "walking around shining like the sun." Consider these sentences Merton wrote in a late essay, published after his death in *Love and Living*, edited by Naomi Burton Stone and Brother Patrick Hart:

> What, then, is the world? Simply the human and non-human environment in which man finds himself, to which he is called to establish a certain definite relationship. It is true that most men are content to accept a ready-made relationship which the world itself offers them, but in theory we are all free to stand back from the world, to judge

it, and even to come to certain decisions about remaking it. (107–8)

Do you think this differs from the way of life and teachings of the Desert Fathers and Mothers?

Lecture 7

Merton describes Gregory of Nyssa's commentary on the Song of Songs, describing "the steps by which the Word makes Himself known to the soul—as a faint 'perfume,' as a voice, and finally as food for the soul that is 'tasted' and sweet." These are such beautiful metaphors.

Are they simply metaphors? Do you ever experience the Beloved in this way? Do you ever hope to experience the Beloved in this way?

Lecture 8

Merton says this about St. Jerome and his legendary short temper: "[W]e have to be careful of taking Jerome as a typical Desert Father. On the whole he is not the best of models for contemplatives. He inspires rather those whose spiritual life is aggressive, ascetical, active, and controversial: but these are often people who stir up monastic orders and cause dissension—though when they are really saints they may accomplish much good."

We all know people like this, don't we? Is there a genuine, completely faithful form of Christian life that is "aggressive" and "controversial"? What do you think?

Lecture 9

Another of the famous Desert Mothers, St. Mary of Egypt, is not mentioned by Merton in this Lecture. She lived in either the early fifth or early sixth century: the sources are indefinite. A prostitute who was so brazen as to join a pilgrimage to Jerusalem in order to offer herself to genuine pilgrims along the way, Mary was barred from entering the Church of the Holy Sepulchre by what she described as a force she couldn't see. Then she saw an icon of the *Theotokos* ("Mother of God") and was suddenly pierced with remorse and repented her sins, deciding to become an ascetic and leave for the desert. She's a character in Goethe's *Faust* and in Mahler's *8th Symphony*.

Each year during Lent, Orthodox Churches read portions of the Life of St. Mary of Egypt, written in the seventh century by St. Sophronius, Patriarch of Jerusalem. It includes the story of Elder Zosima, from a monastery in Palestine, who spends time in the desert, encountering St. Mary there.

> Zosima asked her: "How many years have gone by since you began to live in this desert?" She replied: "Forty-seven years have gone by since I left the holy city." Zosima asked: "But what food do you find?" She said: "I had two-and-a-half loaves when I crossed the Jordan. Soon they dried up and became hard as rock. Eating a little I gradually finished them after a few years." Zosima asked: "Can it be that you have lived so many years this way, without suffering?" The woman answered: "You remind me of what I dare not speak of. For when I recall all the dangers which I overcame, and all the violent thoughts which confused me, I am again afraid that they will take possession of me." Zosima said: "Do not hide anything from me; speak to me without concealing anything."
>
> She went on: "Abba, seventeen years I passed in this desert fighting wild beasts: mad desires and passions. When I was about to partake of food, I used to begin to regret the meat and fish of which I had so much in Egypt. I regretted also not having wine which I loved so much, for I drank a lot of wine when I lived in the world, while here I had not even water. I used to burn and succumb with thirst. The mad desire for profligate songs also entered me

and confused me greatly. But when these desires entered me I struck myself on the breast and reminded myself of the vow I'd made when going into the desert. In my thoughts, I returned to the icon of the Mother of God that had received me and to her I cried in prayer. I implored her to chase away the thoughts. And after weeping for long and beating my breast I used to see light at last which seemed to shine on me from everywhere. And after the violent storm, lasting calm descended."

[Adapted from the version found on the website of St. Mary of Egypt Orthodox Church, Roswell, Georgia: https://www .stmaryofegypt.org/files/library/life.htm.]

Lecture 10

Consider for a moment the Christian saintly tradition of "holy foolishness." Merton writes this, after describing the way of life and spirituality of the stylites:

What attitude should we take toward this kind of sanctity? The fashion has been to disparage it, to treat it as something absurd and grotesque. This is not the full truth. It was a witness to the divine transcendency, and to the superiority of the spirit. Precisely its uselessness was what made this witness powerful.

Do you agree? Do you see any practical application for today?

Lecture 11

When Merton discusses Pseudo-Macarius, he passes over something quickly that merits a pause. He notes that Pseudo-Macarius was not so much Platonist as he was biblical, adding: "This distinction is based on two different views of man. In the former it is the mind, *nous*, that is the seat of spirituality and of prayer."

Consider this quotation from Plato himself, from his *Timaeus*:

> If a man has seriously devoted himself to love of learning and to true wisdom . . . then there is absolutely no way that his thoughts can fail to be immortal and divine. . . . And to the extent that human nature can partake of immortality, he can in no way fail to achieve this.

[From *Timaeus*, 90 b-c, Donald J. Zehl, trans., *Plato: Complete Works*, ed. John M. Cooper and D. S. Hutchinson (Indianapolis: Hackett Publishing Company, 1997).]

1. For Plato, the *nous* of intelligence is the part of the soul most apt to reach the Divine. To Merton's point, what is the biblical view?

2. How do you think your intelligence and your heart/soul work together to reach to, or respond to, God?

Lecture 12

Describing Evagrius's teaching from *On Prayer*, Merton writes: "*Apatheia* is the victory of the soul over all the devils (i.e., all the passions). Note that *apatheia* is not mere insensibility. It is compounded of humility, compunction, zeal, and intense love for God."

At the end of the long paragraph in which this clarification from Merton occurs, he adds: "Note that prayer is inseparably connected with virtue. Without virtue, one cannot resist passion, and if one is dominated by passion, he has no control of thoughts and cannot pray."

1. How might these two, *apatheia* and virtue, come together in the ideal Christian life?

2. Do they interact in your own spiritual life and practice?

Lecture 13

In his book *The Wisdom of the Desert* (1960), Merton wrote:

> The flight to the desert was neither purely negative nor purely individualistic. They were not rebels against society. . . . They were men who did not believe in letting themselves be passively guided and ruled by a decadent state, and who believed that there was a way of getting along without slavish dependence on accepted, conventional values. . . . They did not reject society with proud contempt. . . . The society they sought was one where all men were truly equal, where the only authority under God was the charismatic authority of wisdom, experience and love. . . . What the Fathers sought most of all was their own true self, in Christ. (5)

Do you see the Desert Fathers and Mothers, and the way and practice of faith as found in desert spirituality, relevant for your life in the twenty-first century?

Lecture 14

When discussing Conference 9, in which Abbot Isaac turns to different types of prayer, Merton summarizes:

> The first difficulty in explaining the "kinds of prayer" is that there is in reality an almost infinite variety. Prayer is always varying. It is a living reality and there are as many kinds of prayer as there are variations of spiritual states. . . . Abbot Isaac reminds us that we pray differently under different circumstances, and in "classifying" prayer we must not forget these differences and these potential variations. In other words, we must not bind ourselves to pray always in the same way, or expect our prayer to fall always into the same pattern. We must not impose a rigid plan on our prayer life and try to make life conform to an abstract theory of our own, but we must on the contrary let our

prayer be living, and let it grow out of our life in union with God.

Is this word from the desert father useful in your life? Why or why not?

Lecture 15

Merton summarizes Philoxenos in Homily 4 about Adam and Eve in the Garden:

> Adam and Eve before the Fall knew nothing of "worldly affairs"—which were simply irrelevant to their state. God was always with them, taking them wherever they went. He showed them everything from near at hand like a man. And they received no thought about Him in their Spirit. They never asked: Where does He live who shows us these things? How long has He existed? And if He created all else, was He also created? And we, why has He created us? Why has He placed us in this Paradise? Why has He given us this Law?

Do you feel it's better that we ask these questions today? Why or why not?

Finally, one of the joys of reading Merton are the ways his spiritual teaching reflect, deliberately as well as inadvertently, his biography. To those who know Merton's biography, reflect on this passage from the second half of the lecture on Philoxenos:

> Philoxenos emphasizes the importance of interior silence— calming down before trying seriously to pray. The new man is a "man of silence"—there is a relationship of silence and joy. But again there are two levels: by grace (of the Sacrament) one puts on the new man but does not experience this silence; by the practice of joy one experiences the silence of the Spirit. This means getting rid of all the old man by renunciation, and putting on all the new man, made in

the likeness of God. If one does not completely renew himself in Christ, the old man becomes merely "the tomb in which the new man is buried." (Conflicts of monastic life are due to this!)

Do you experience this conflict in your life? In your relationships?

Editor's Notes

he original, unabridged versions of thirteen of these lectures were first published in Thomas Merton, *Cassian and the Fathers: Initiation into the Monastic Tradition*, edited by Patrick F. O'Connell (Trappist, KY: Cistercian Publications, 2005). Two of those thirteen, "Aberrations in the Early Centuries" and "Palestinian Monasticism and St. Jerome," also include material from *Pre-Benedictine Monasticism: Initiation into the Monastic Tradition 2*, edited by Patrick F. O'Connell (Kalamazoo, MI: Cistercian Publications, 2006), and two of the lectures here—"The Community of St. Melania" and "Philoxenos of Mabbug"—come entirely from that latter book.

I have done abridgements throughout, and the result is a book that differs substantially from O'Connell's scholarly work. My task has been mostly to pare the talks down to more digestible size. Occasionally, I have replaced a Latin quotation that Merton read, and which appeared in his typescript, with O'Connell's English translation. At other times, I have retained an O'Connell footnote, but often in edited form, and then credited to him. O'Connell's added words in brackets, to supplement the shorthand of Merton's transcript, have been incorporated into the whole; on very few occasions, I have changed a word from those added in brackets, and then incorporated all, from what O'Connell provided in the scholarly editions. Other editing on my part includes changing certain instances of shorthand in the manuscript, for instance changing "v.g." to "for example," and "n.b." to "note well," for the sake of the average reader. Occasionally, I found it necessary to break up a long paragraph into two, or to add a new heading or subheading. Occasional editorial additions of my own, which appear rarely, are in brackets [ ]. Any other changes are noted below.

Preface: Combines passages from two places in the original type-script. The first part comes from the opening of what Merton called his "Prologue to Cassian"; the second part is taken from the portion of typescript presented here as Lecture 9.

Lecture 2: The section "Hatred of the Flesh" includes portions of a lecture on St. Basil from *Pre-Benedictine Monasticism: Initiation into the Monastic Tradition 2* (pp. 126–28), and portions of a lecture on Syrian and Persian Monasticism; see pages 216–18 of that book.

Lecture 8: Twice in the opening paragraph, I silently changed Merton's use of the outdated "monachism" to "monasticism." This same change is made on a few other occasions throughout the whole.

The section "Jerome's Monastic Doctrine" includes several paragraphs from *Pre-Benedictine Monasticism: Initiation into the Monastic Tradition 2*; see pages 162–64 of that book.

Lecture 11: Some small editorial fixes here; for instance, changing Merton's Isaac of "Niniveh" to Isaac of Nineveh.

Index